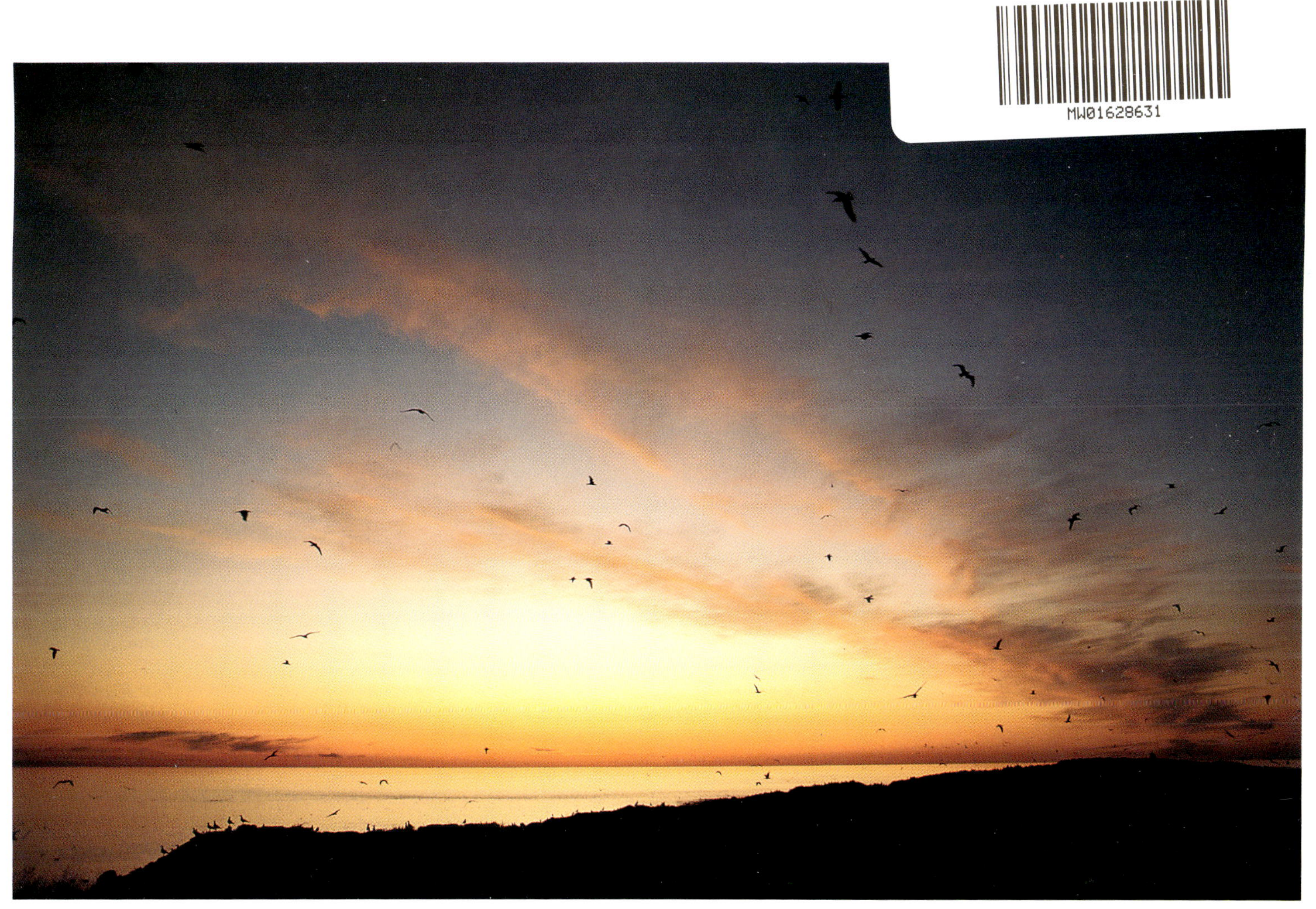

MW01628631

Out On The Shoals

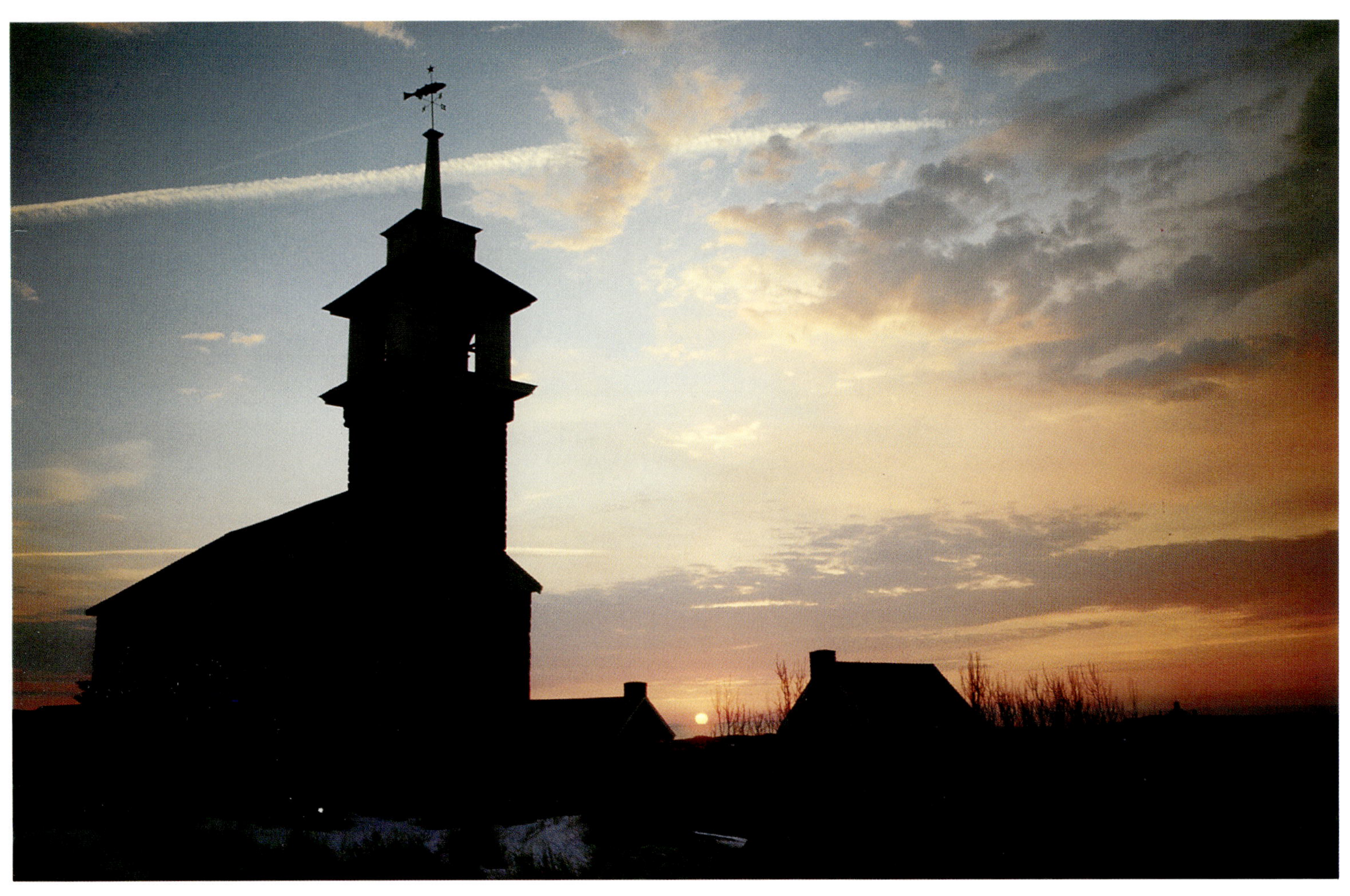

A February sunrise on Star Island. (preceeding page) Sunrise from Smuttynose.

Out On The Shoals

Twenty Years of Photography
On the Isles of Shoals

Peter E. Randall

Peter E. Randall Publisher
Portsmouth
1995

To Judy

Printed and bound in Hong Kong.

Peter E. Randall Publisher
Box 4726, Portsmouth, NH 03802

ISBN 0914339-52-4

Front cover: Herring gulls and Star Island from Appledore.

Rear cover: Main islands of the Isles of Shoals, looking south. Clockwise from top: White and Seavey, Lunging, Appledore, Smuttynose (with Malaga on its western end), Cedar, and Star. Duck, not shown, would be about under the airplane from which this photograph was taken.

Introduction

"Where's Peter," they'd ask, and for some twenty years, my wife Judy would reply, "Out on the Shoals."

Almost everyone has a special place and for me it has been the Isles of Shoals, a group of nine small islands off the coast of New Hampshire and Maine. Rich in history, diverse in social atmosphere, and ruggedly beautiful, these islands have called to me many times since the mid-1970s when I first aimed my camera at the rocky shores and the spectacular birds I found there.

Since my first trip one spring with University of New Hampshire Professor Art Borror and his ornithology class, I have returned countless times in all seasons to visit every island, photographing primarily with 35mm cameras, shooting mainly color slides. My first efforts resulted in a small booklet called *On This Coast*, portraying my work and the photographs of Bill Finney of Concord, New Hampshire. Later my photographs were selected for inclusion in a now famous University of New Hampshire exhibit called "A Stern and Lovely Scene." Renowned Durham painter John Hatch and I were the only living artists to be represented.

Next came the small guidebook, *All Creation and the Isles of Shoals*. I thought that book of photographs, now out of print, would complete my work on the islands, but I was drawn back again and again, and my body of work continued to grow. Collections of photographs have appeared in many regional and national magazines. Not long ago I realized that two decades had passed since beginning my work on the islands. After twenty of years, it seemed appropriate to offer a new presentation of my efforts.

Everywhere I have turned during the past twenty years, someone has been willing to assist me in my quest to photograph the Shoals. The list of helpers and supporters is too long to write here, and, perhaps, I have forgotten a few names, but without all them, this book would not have happened. Several people deserve special mention, however. Through the support of John Kingsbury and J. B. Heiser, former directors of the Shoals Marine Laboratory, I spent much time on Appledore, making my own photographs, but also giving lectures and directing several nature photography workshops.

Star Island friends Fred McGill and Betty Lockwood saw to it that I visited that island to give lectures and conduct photography workshops, while adding to my own work. My wife and three children accompanied me to the islands many times, but mostly I went alone and they waited at home for my return. So for friends and supporters, and for my family, this new volume is my way of saying, "Thank you."

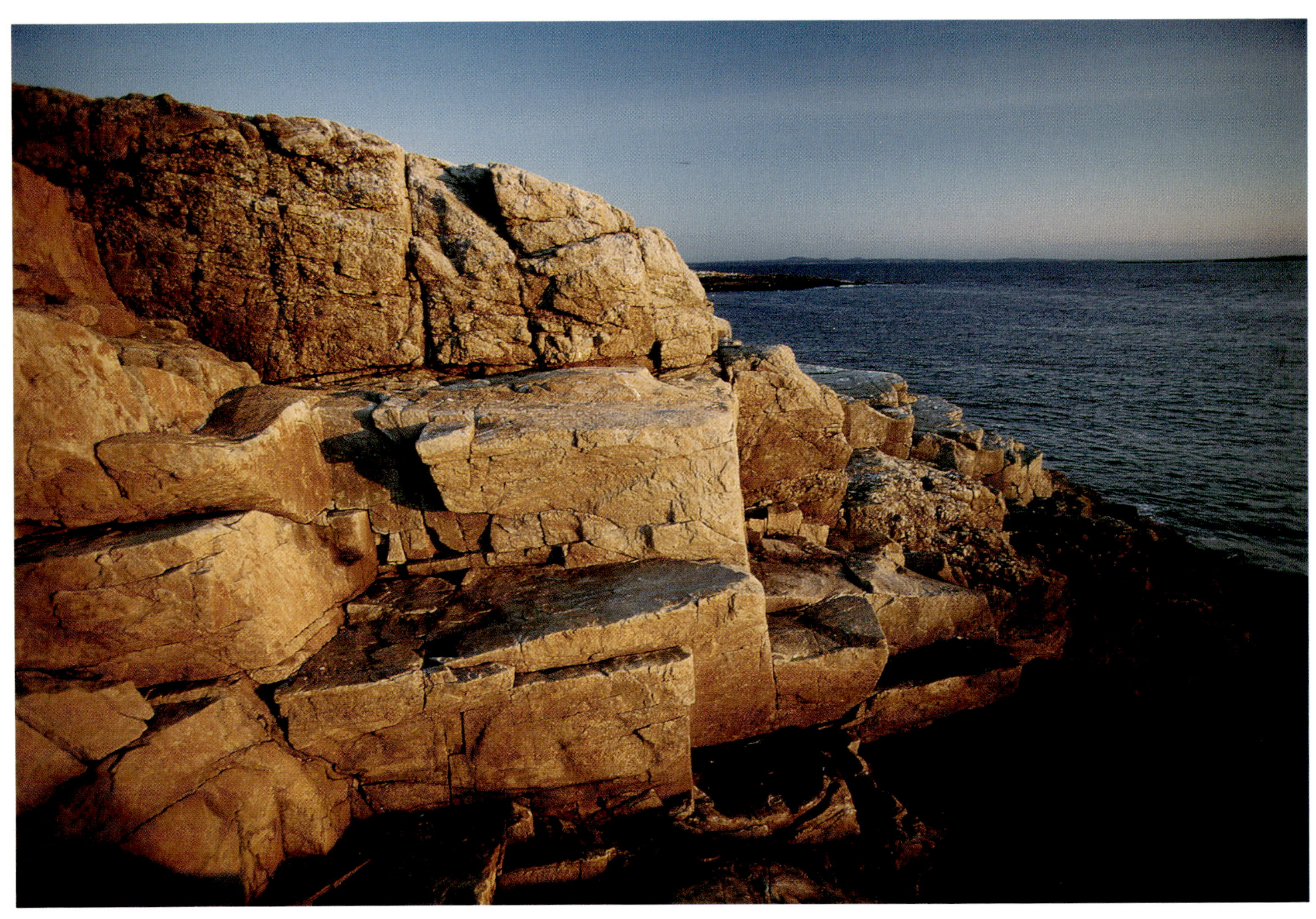

6 Early morning light, Appledore.

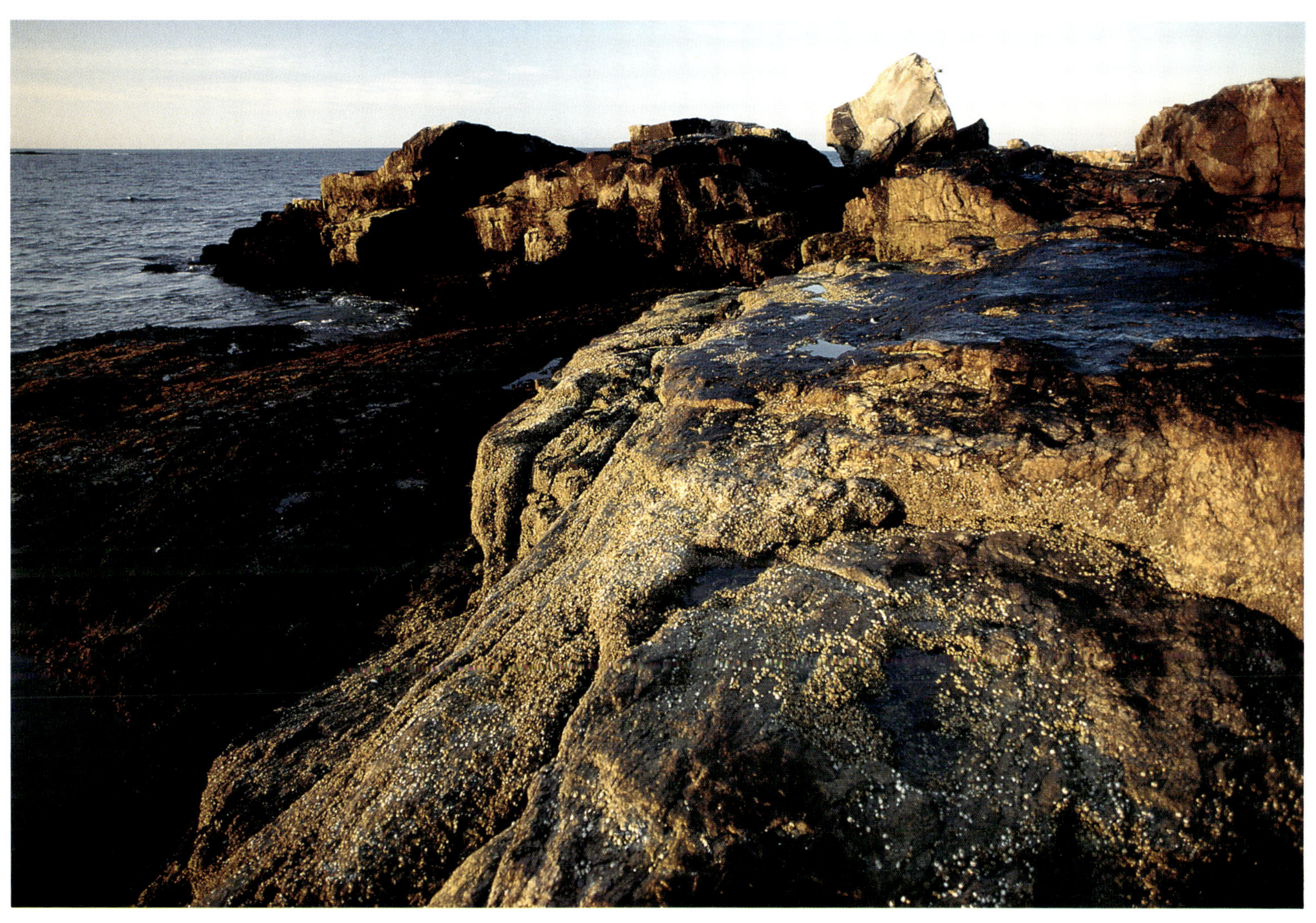

Morning light, Smuttynose. In the background is pointed Maren's Rock. When murderer Louis Wagner rowed from the mainland to Smuttynose in March 1873 and killed two women while attempting a robbery, a third woman, Maren Honvet, survived by walking barefoot the length of the island and hiding under this rock.

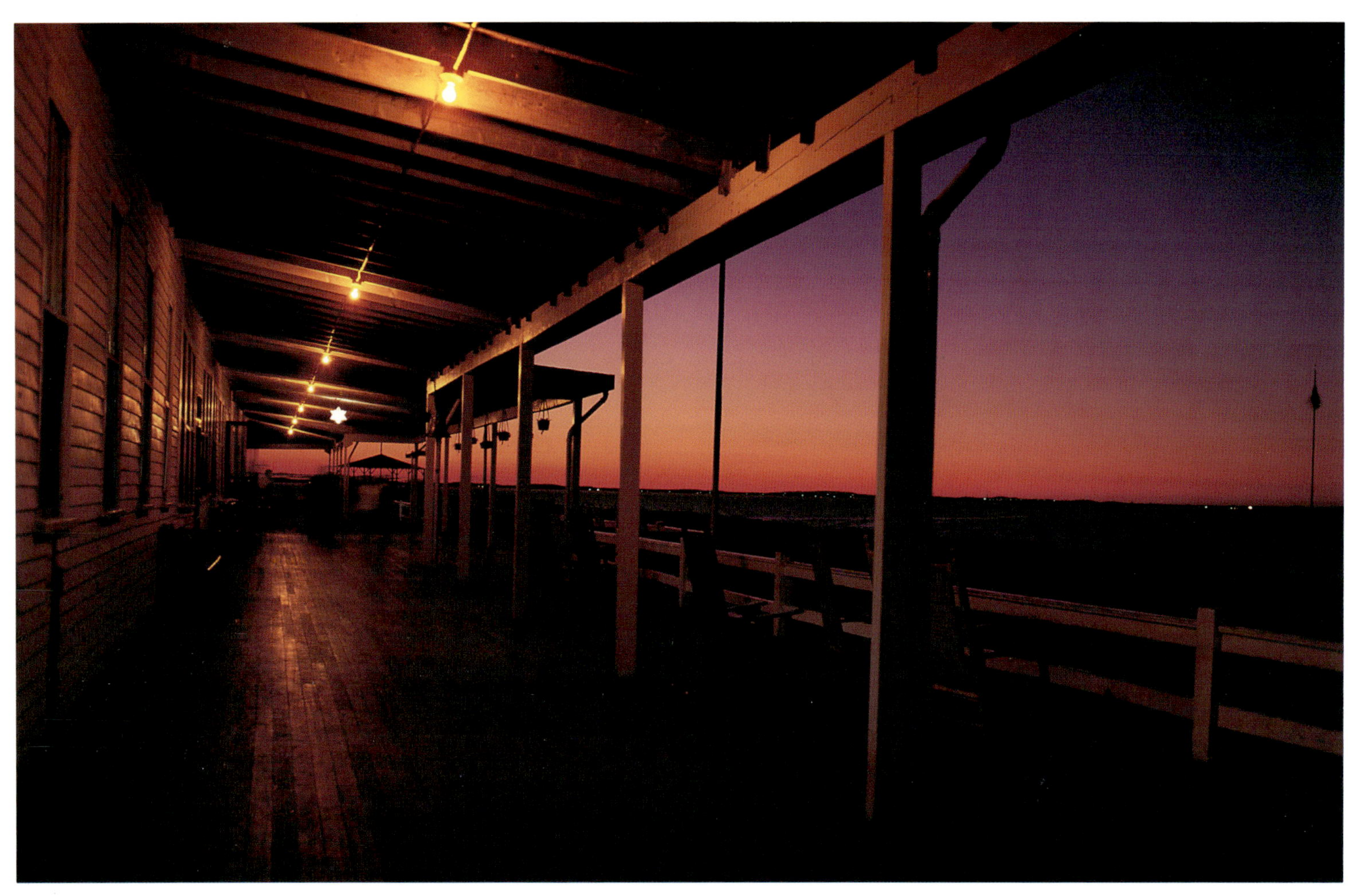

 Before dawn, front porch, Oceanic Hotel, Star Island.

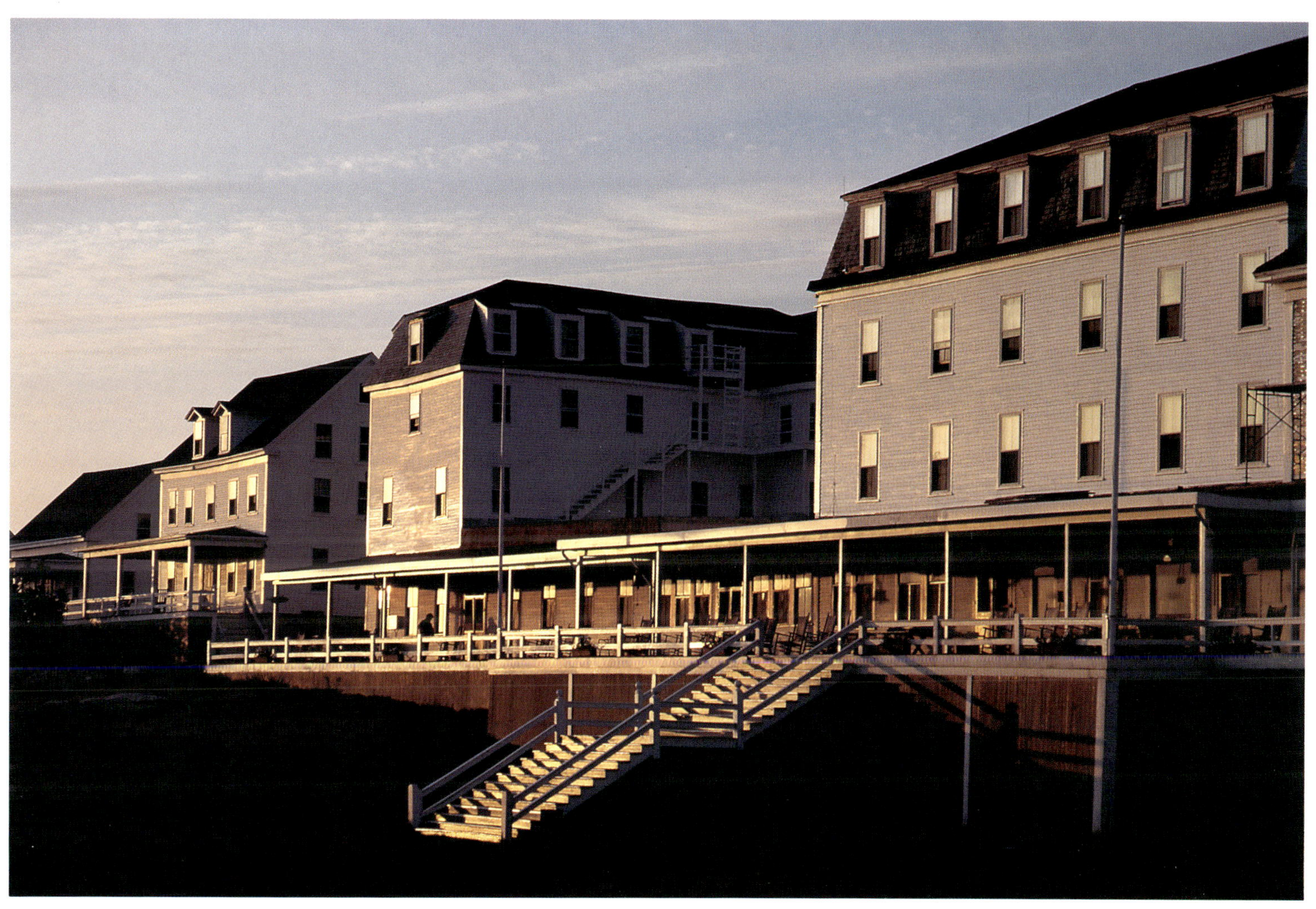

Morning light, Oceanic Hotel, Star Island.

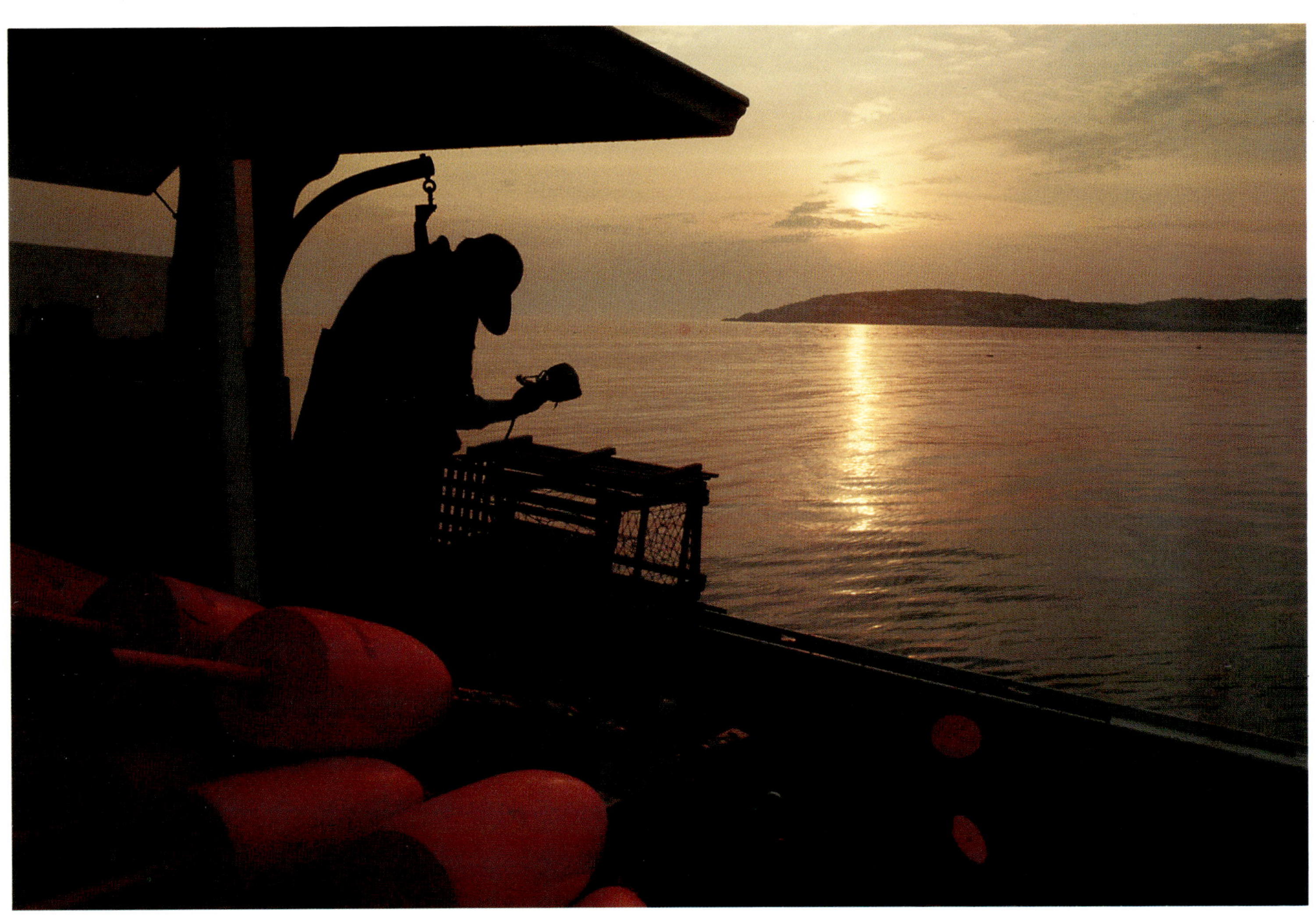

 Lobsterman Rodney Sullivan fishing off Appledore.

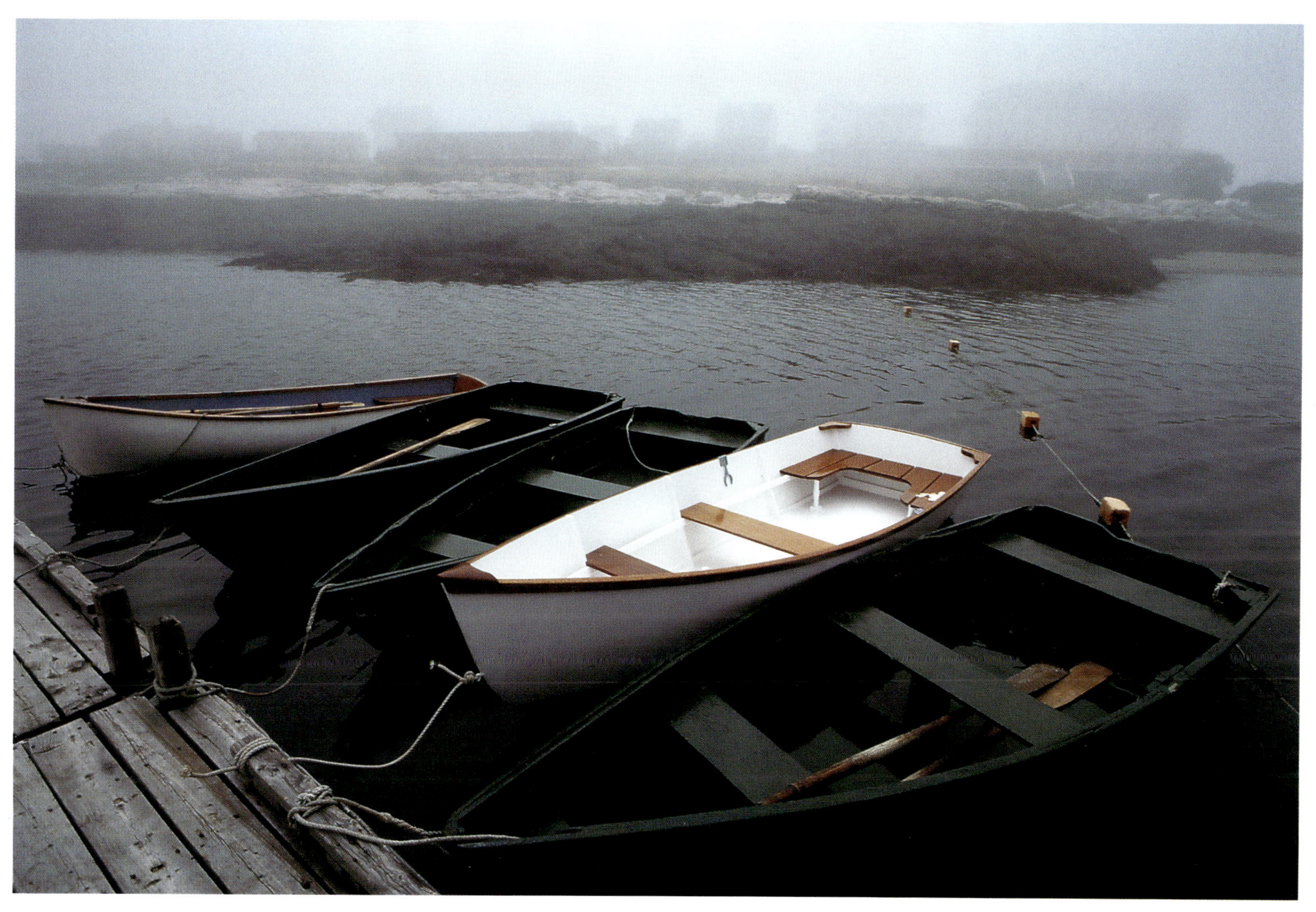

Morning fog, Star Island.

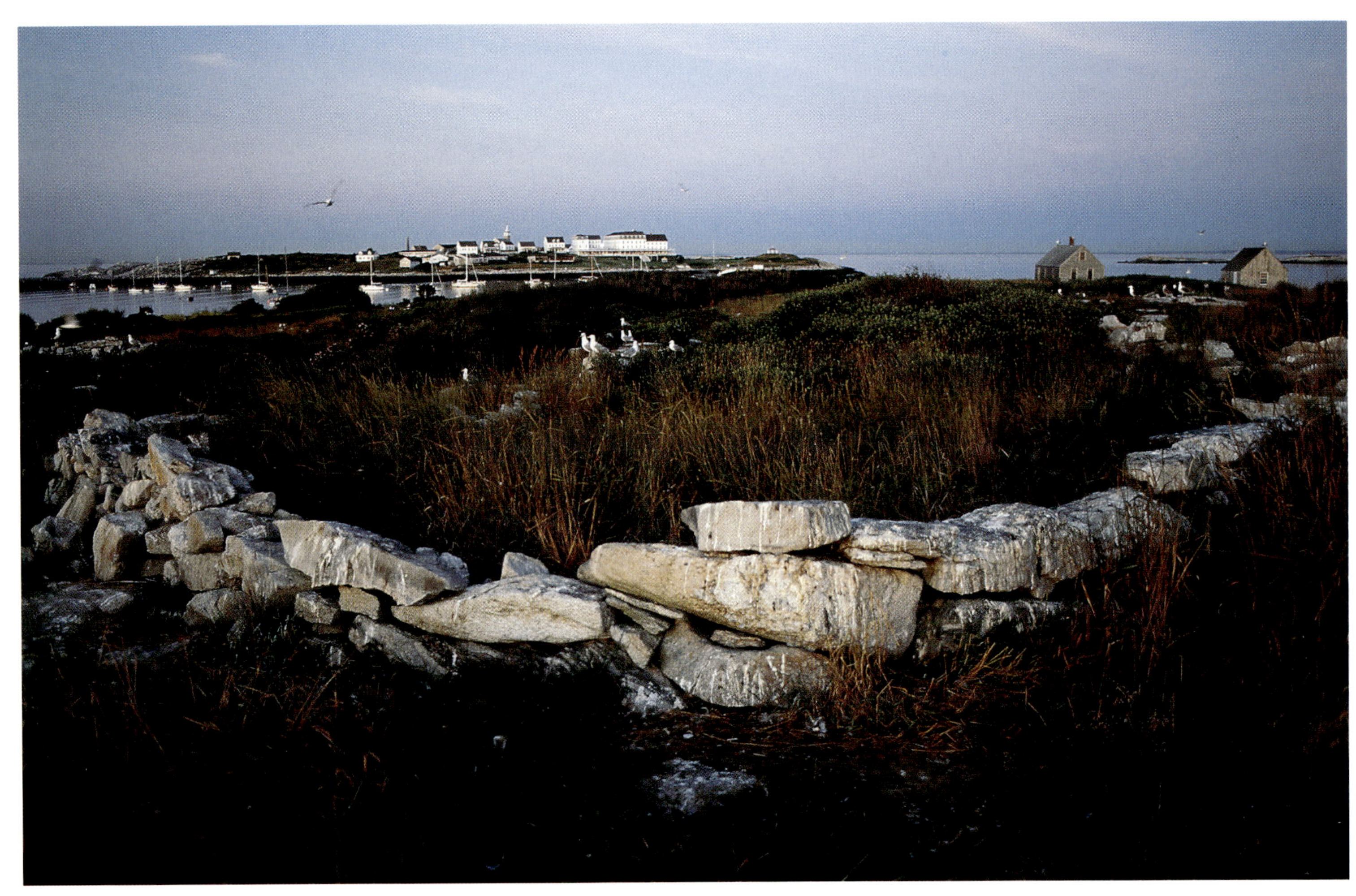

12 Curved wall, Smuttynose.

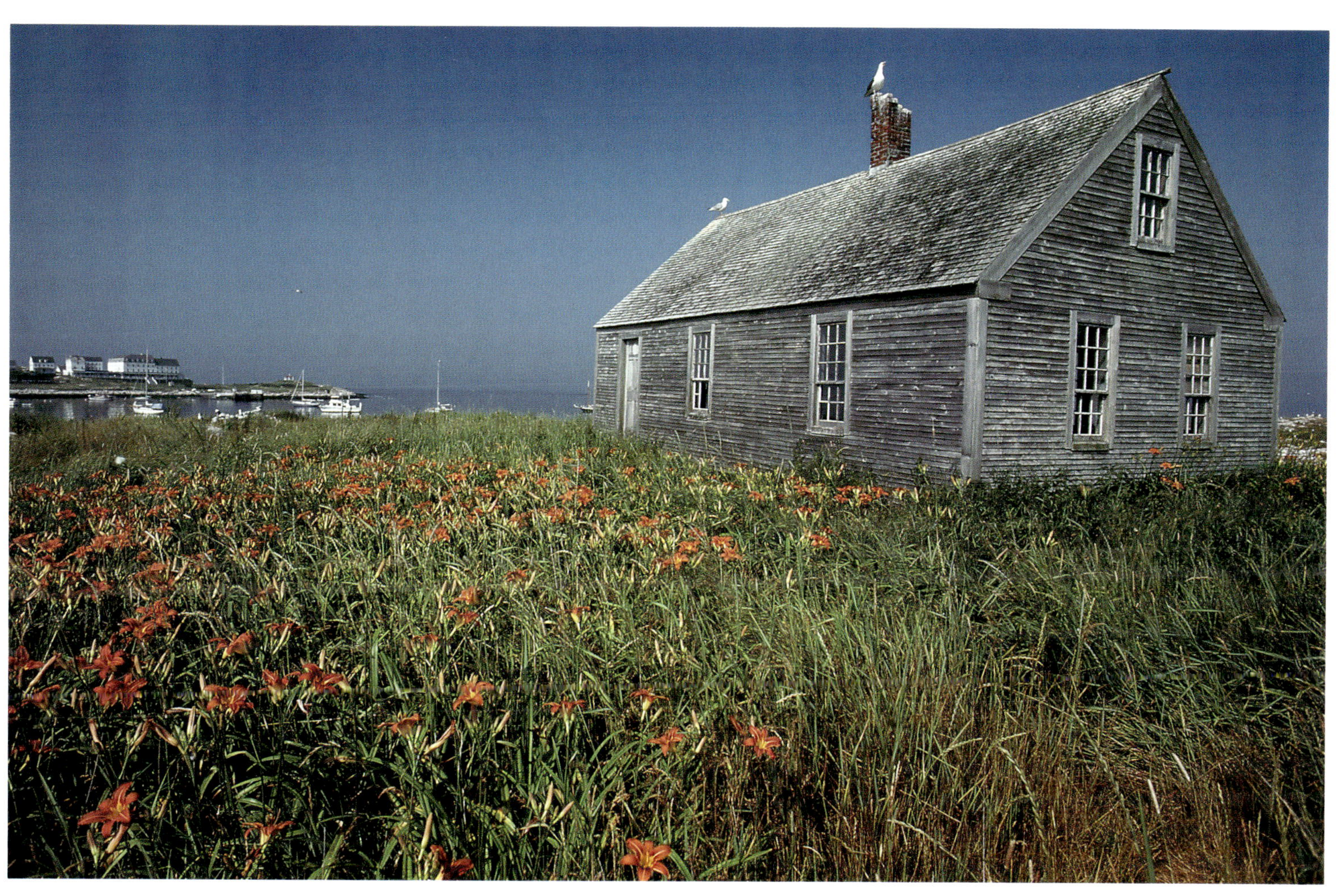

Mid summer morning, Haley House, Smuttynose.

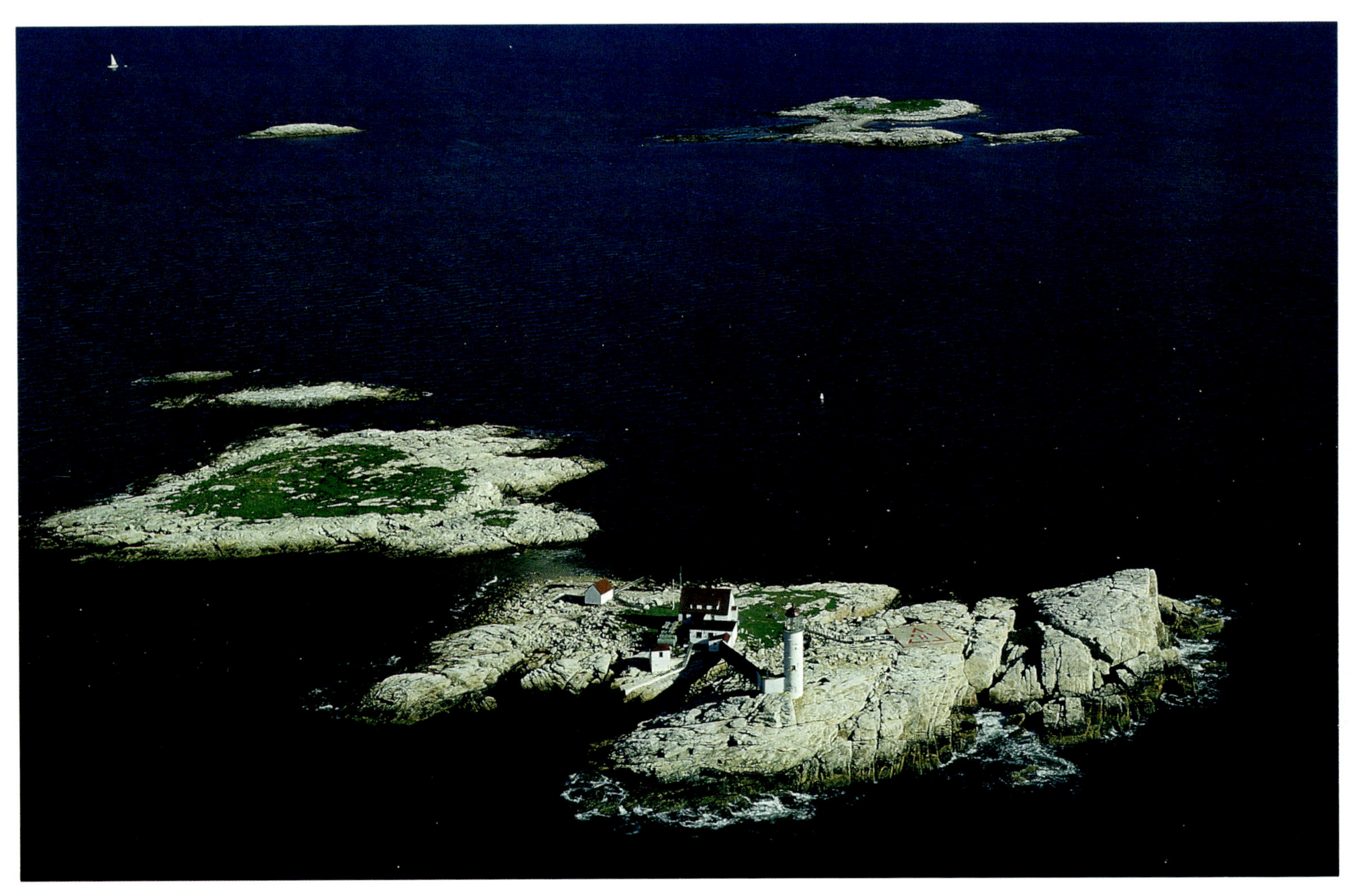

 White and Seavey islands, with Lunging in the background, Square Rock at left.

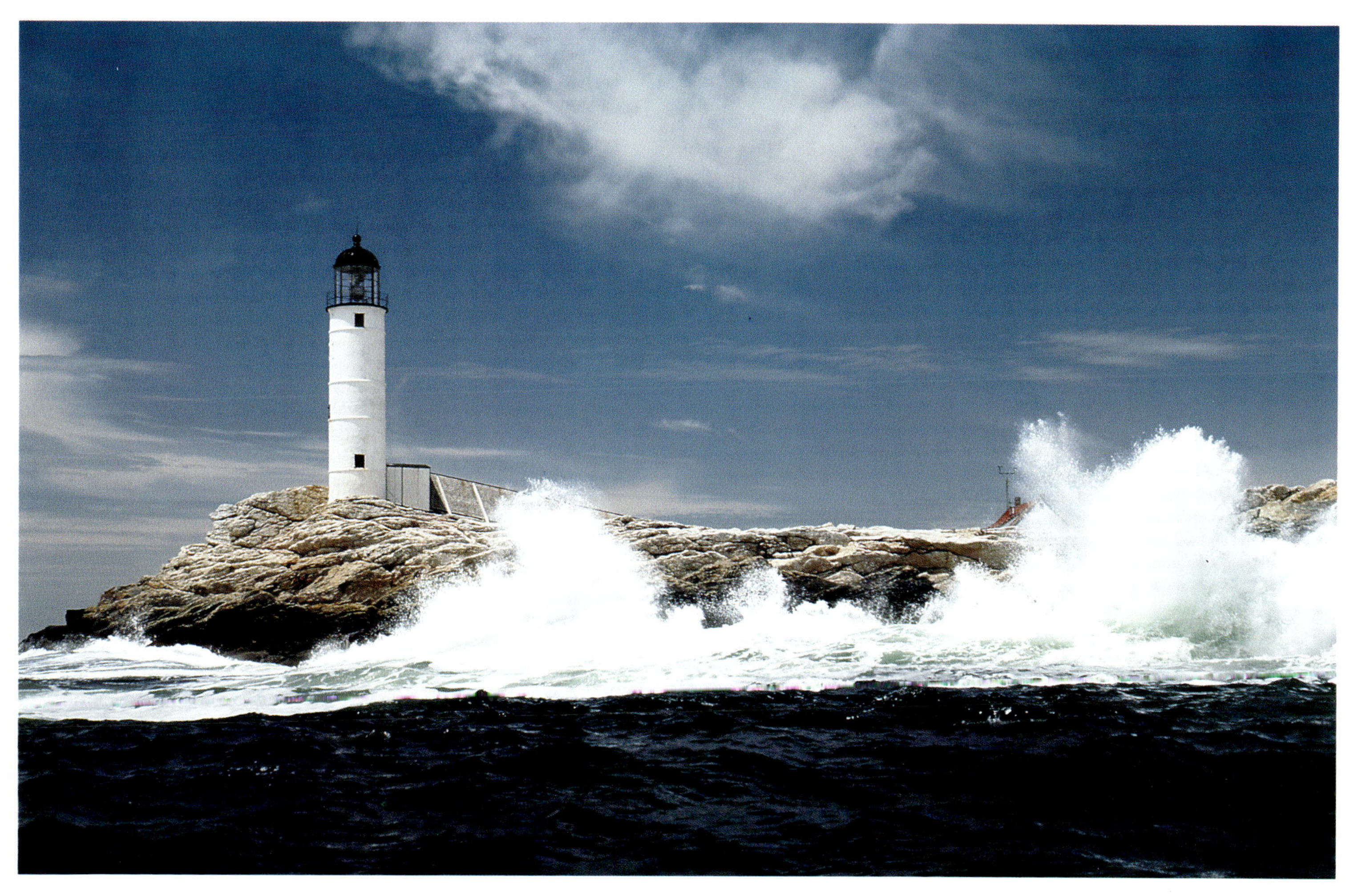

White Island Light.

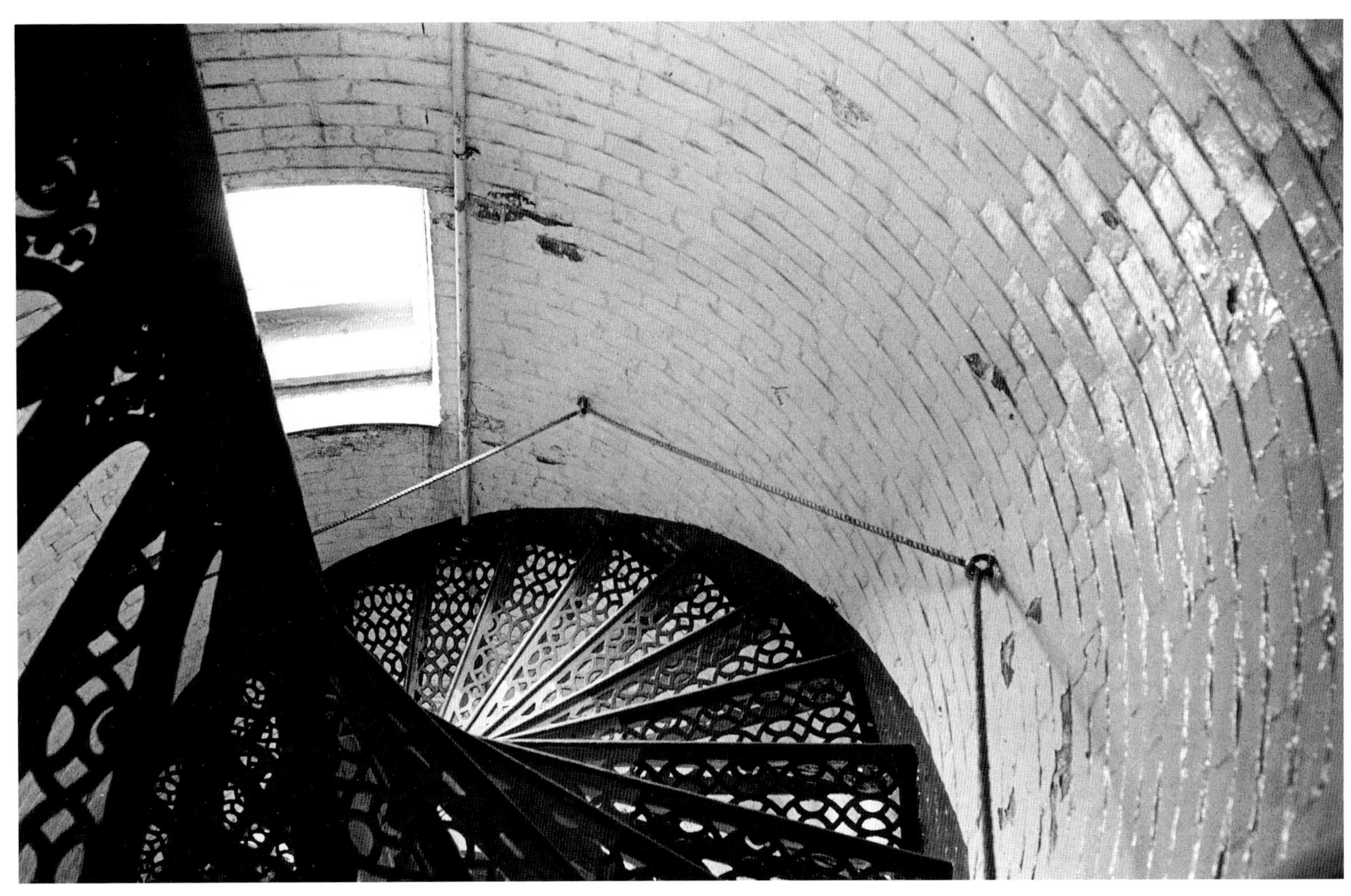

 Inside the lighthouse tower, White Island.

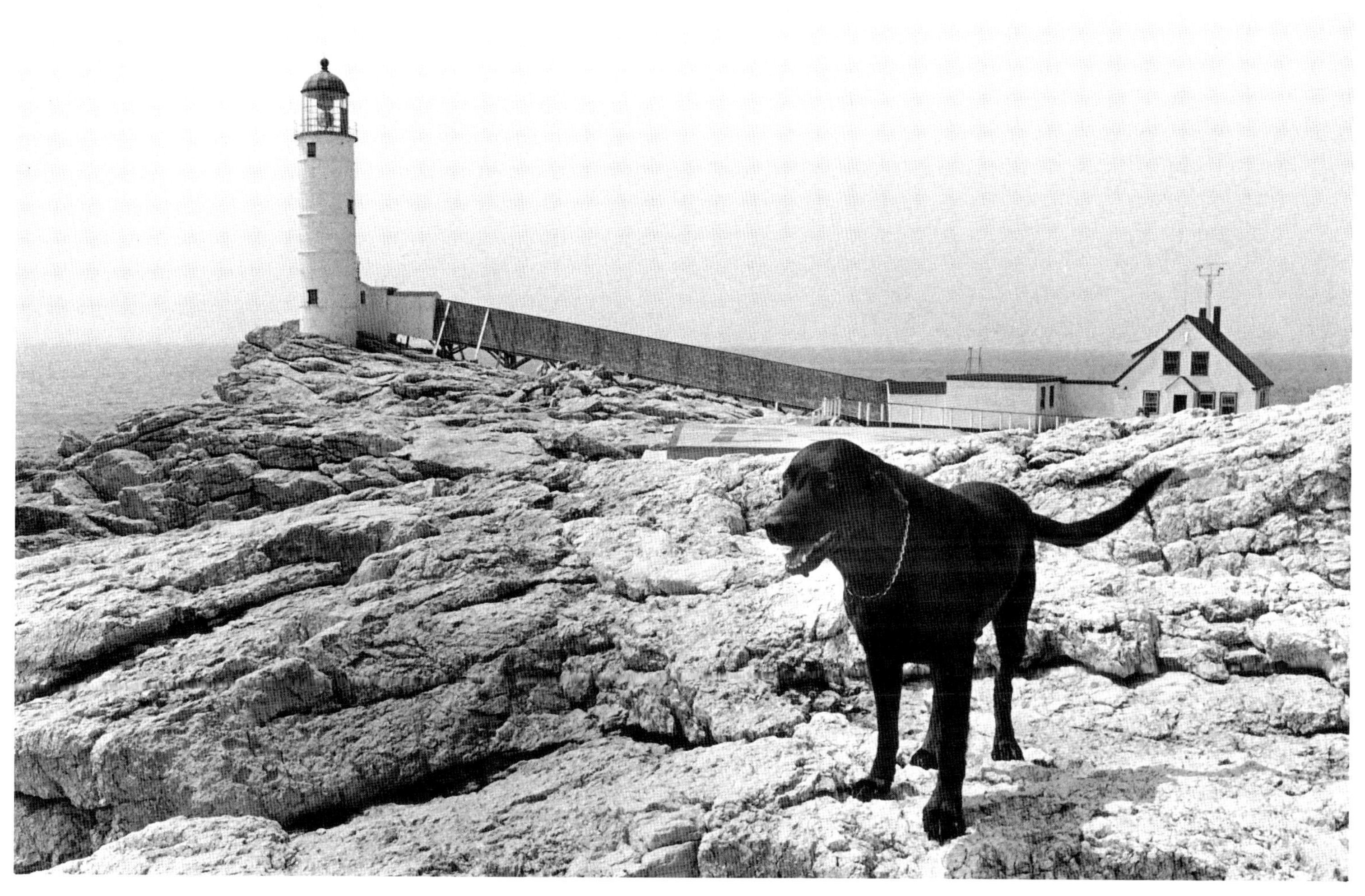

Shoals, the lighthouse dog, lived on White Island for 15 years when Coast Guard personnel operated the lighthouse. The light is now solar-powered and the island is unocupied.

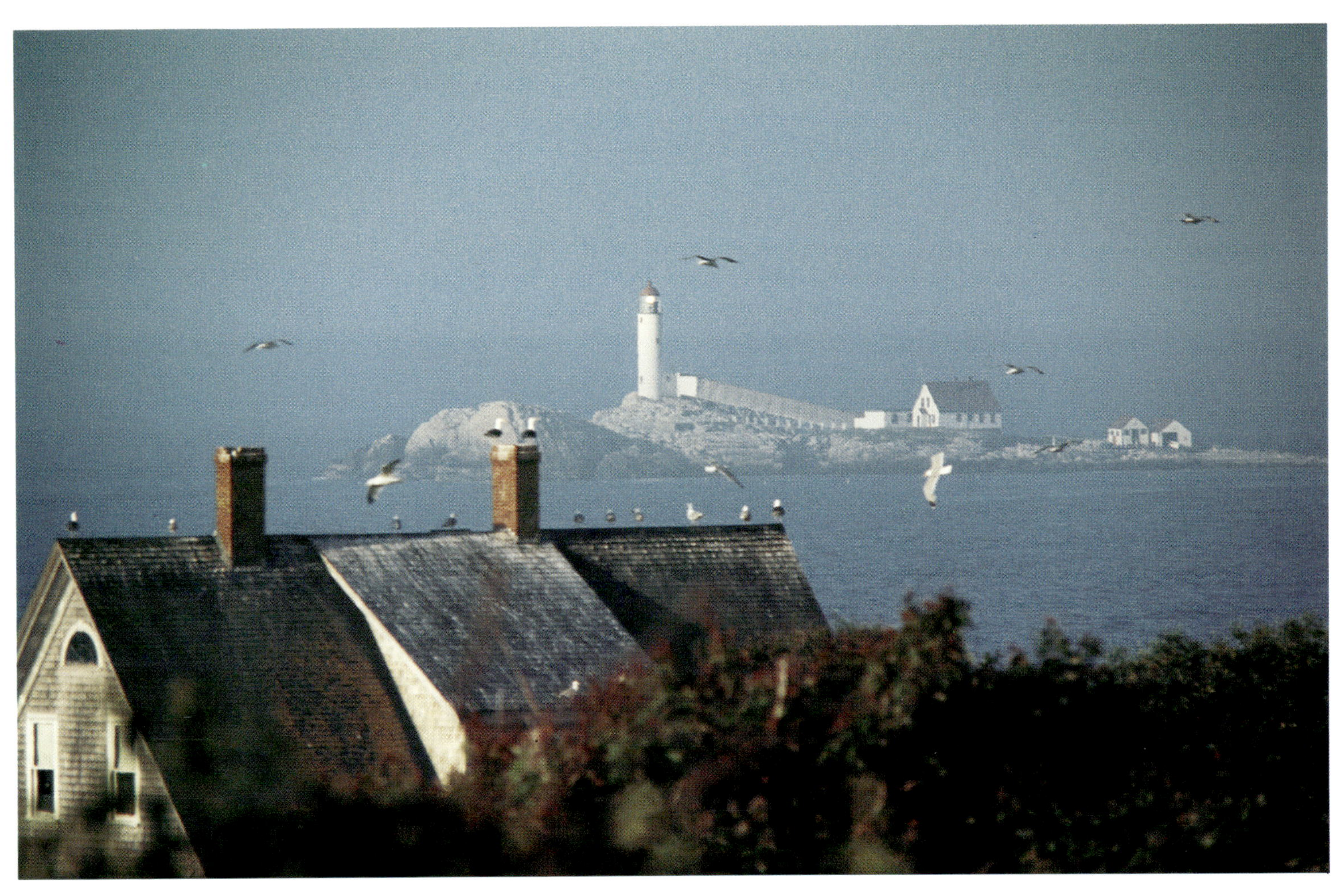

18 White Island from Appledore.

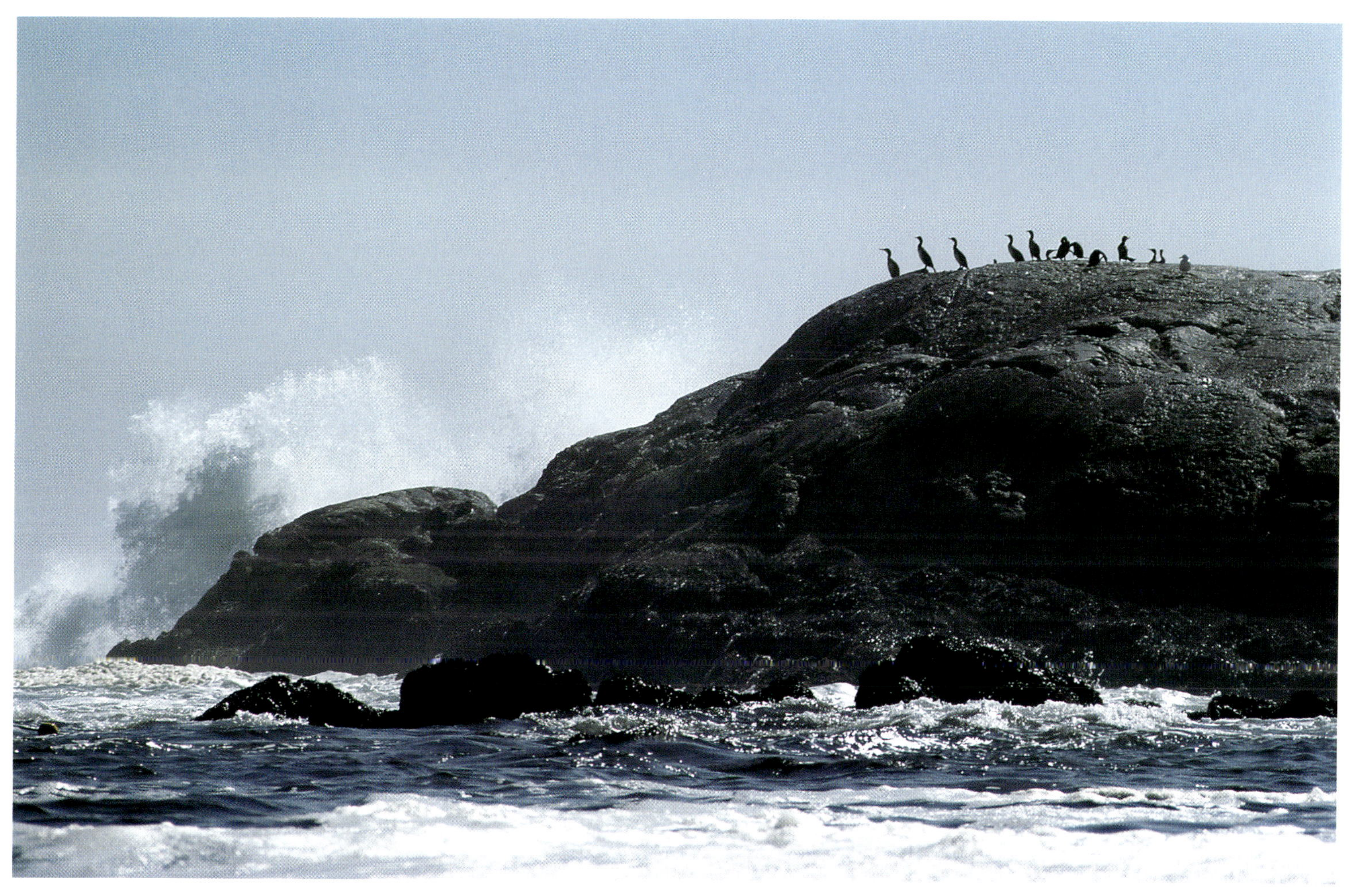

Cormorants, Duck Island.

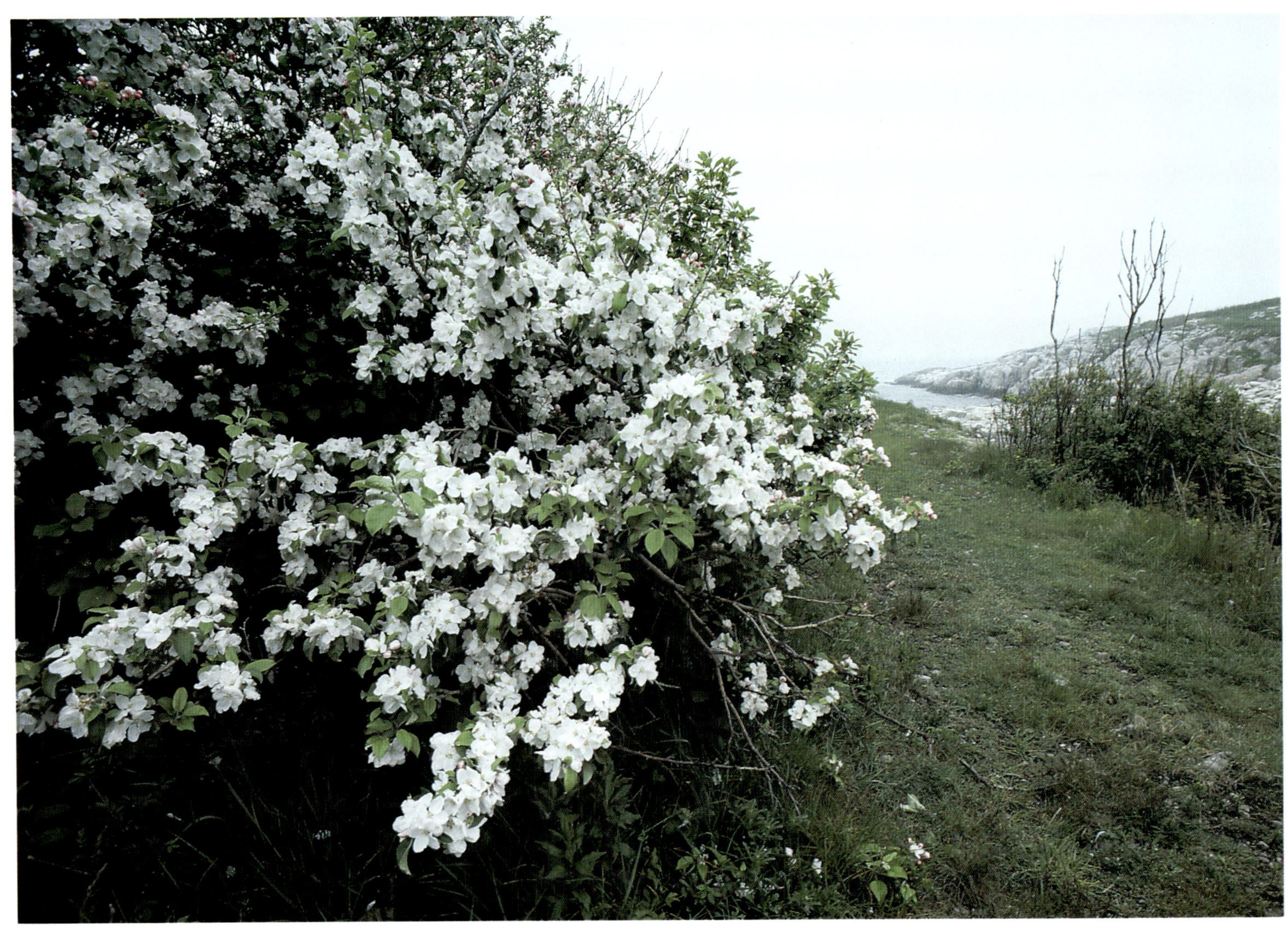

20 Apple blossoms, Broad Cove, Appledore.

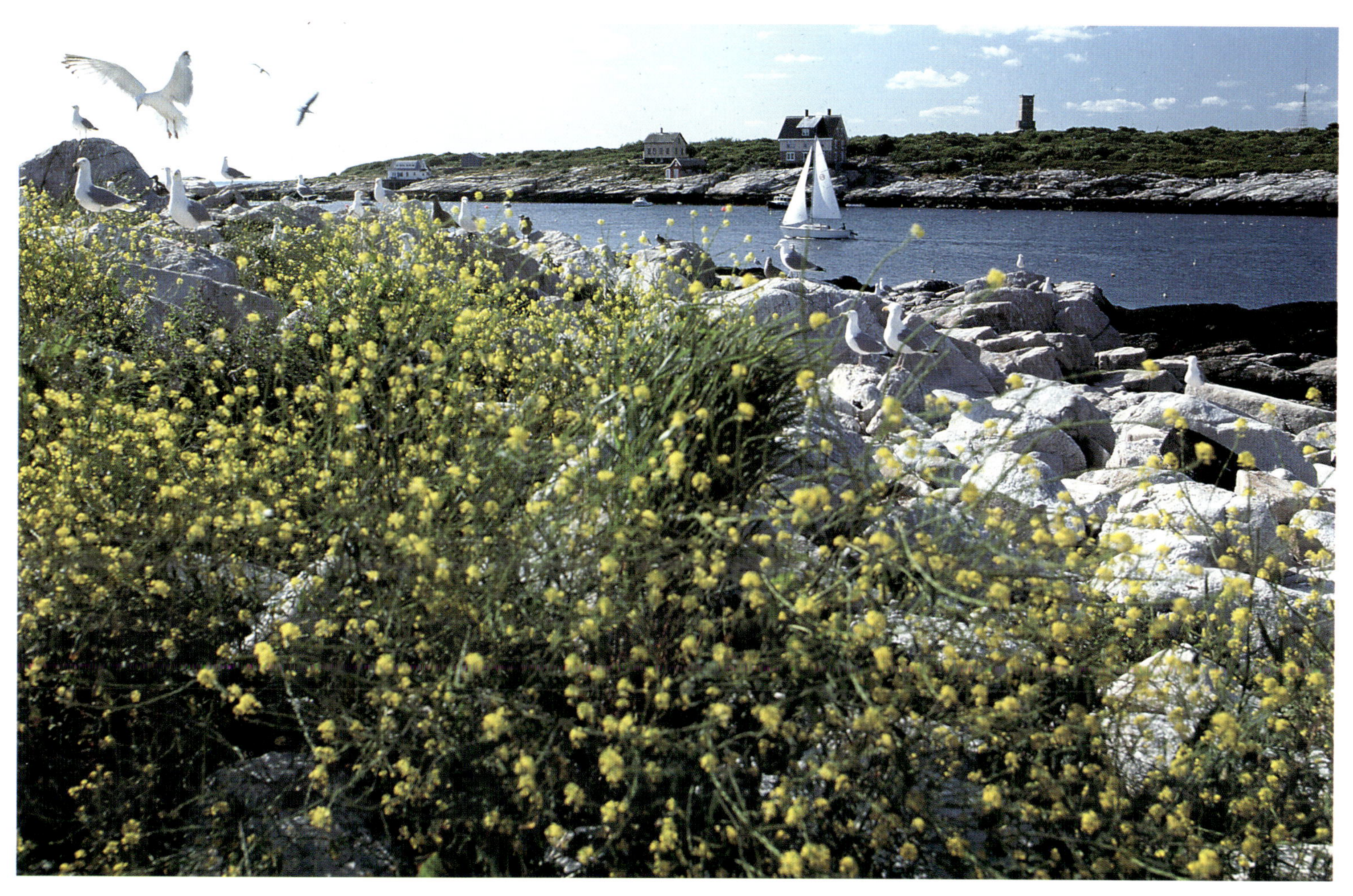

Appledore from Smuttynose.

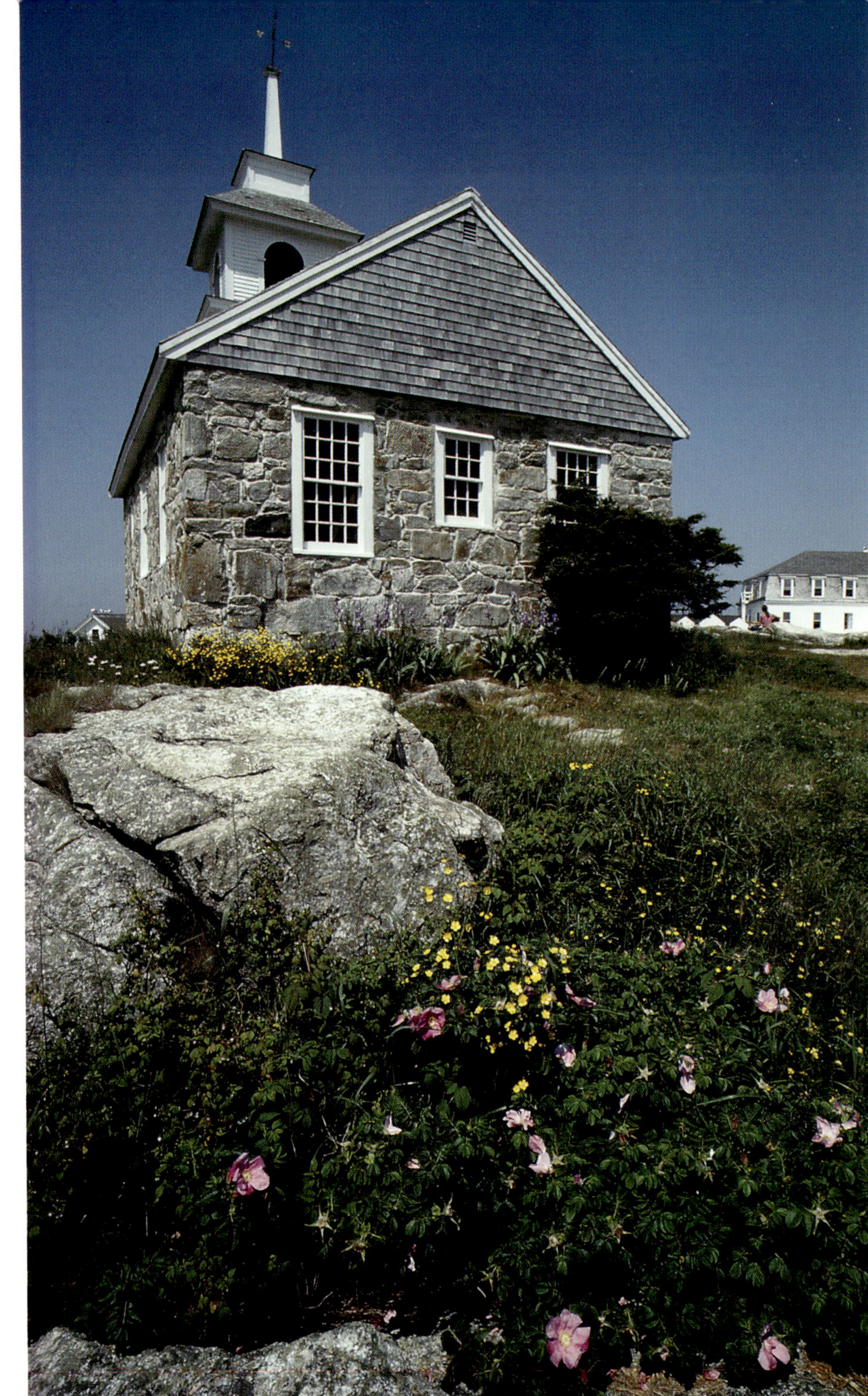

22 Gosport Church, Star Island.

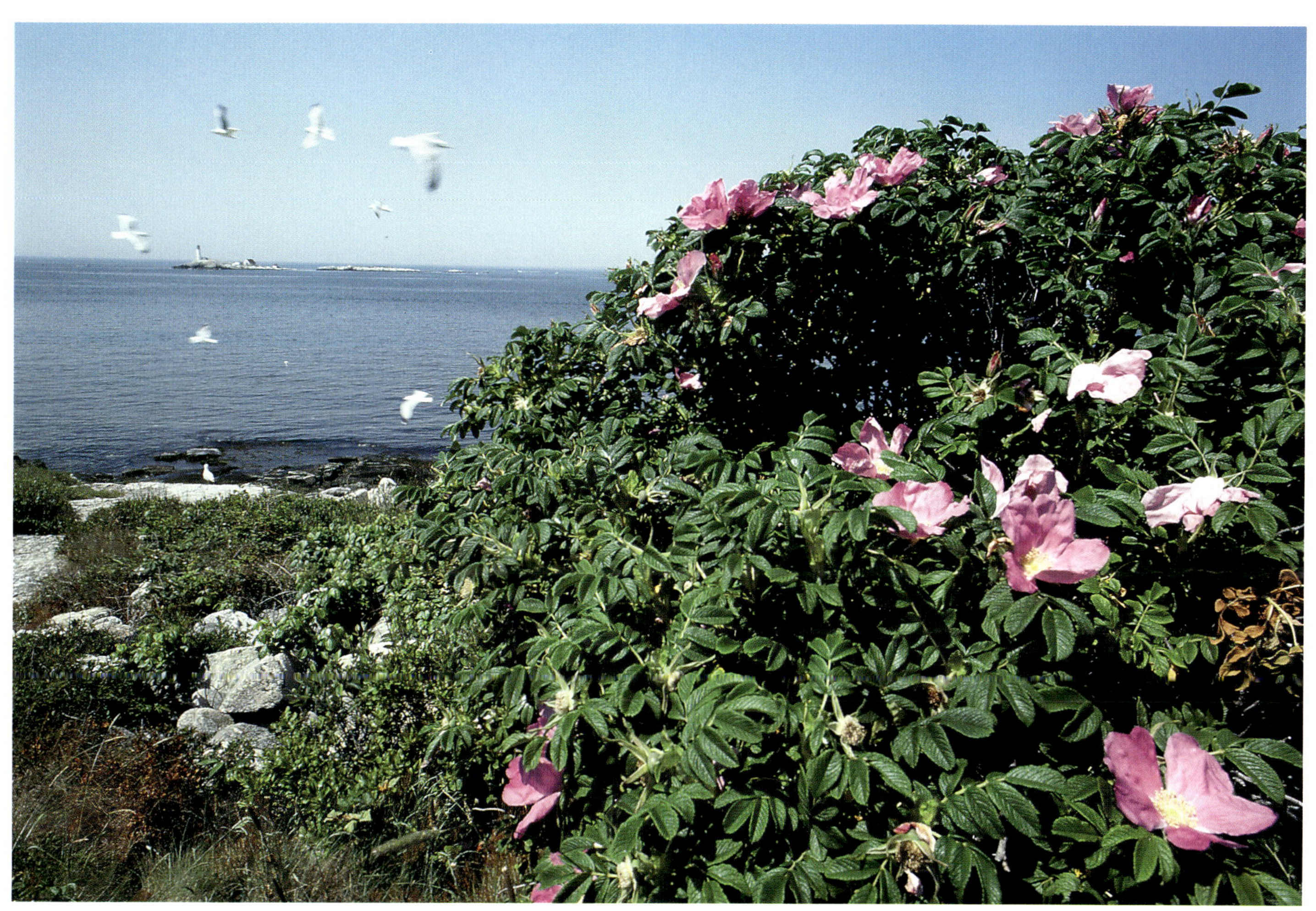

Sea roses and White Island, from Star Island.

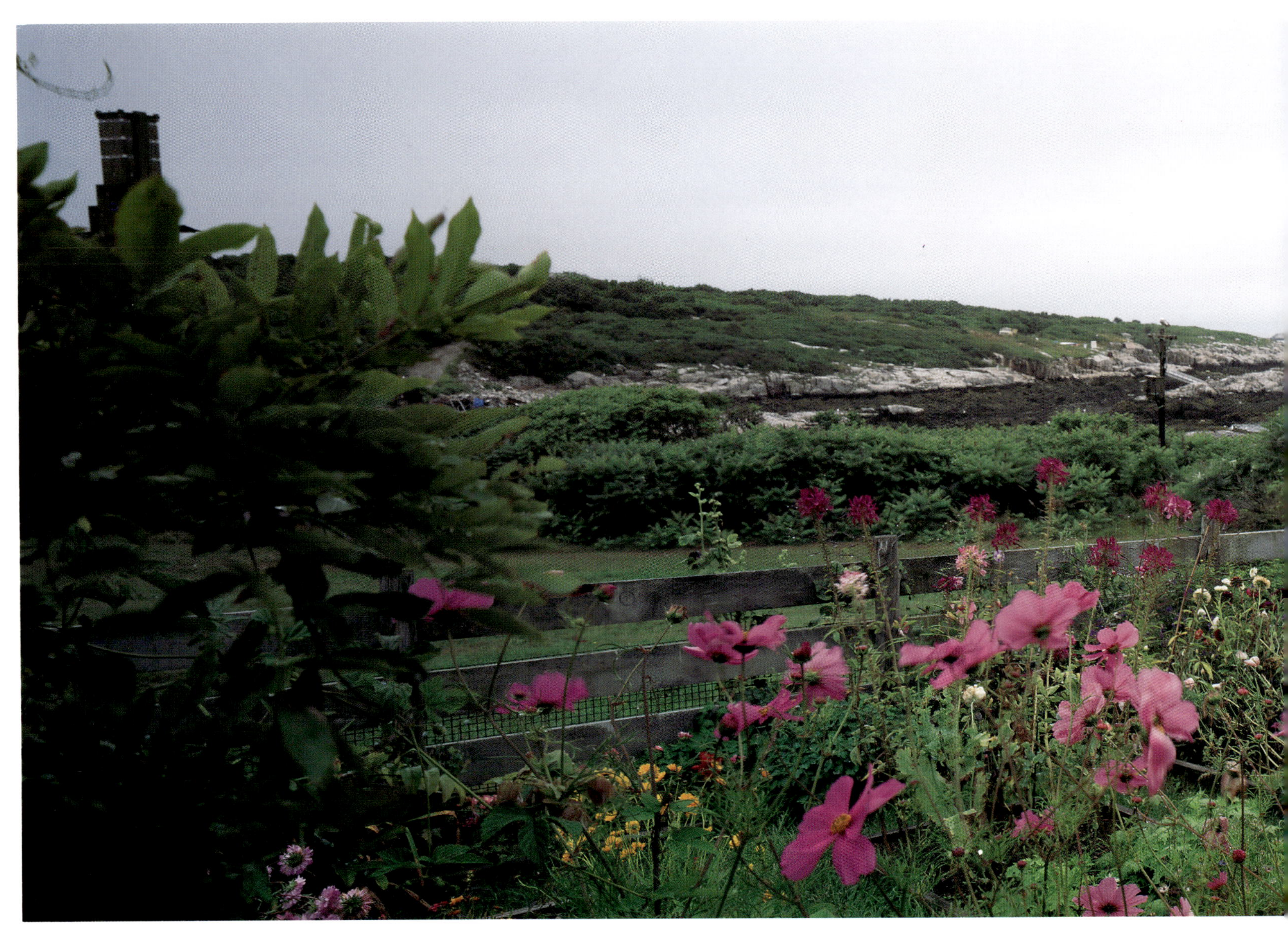

24 Celia Thaxter's garden, Appledore. The Shoals Marine Laboratory re-established Celia's famous island garden in 1977 and it is now maintained by volunteers from the mainland and lab staff.

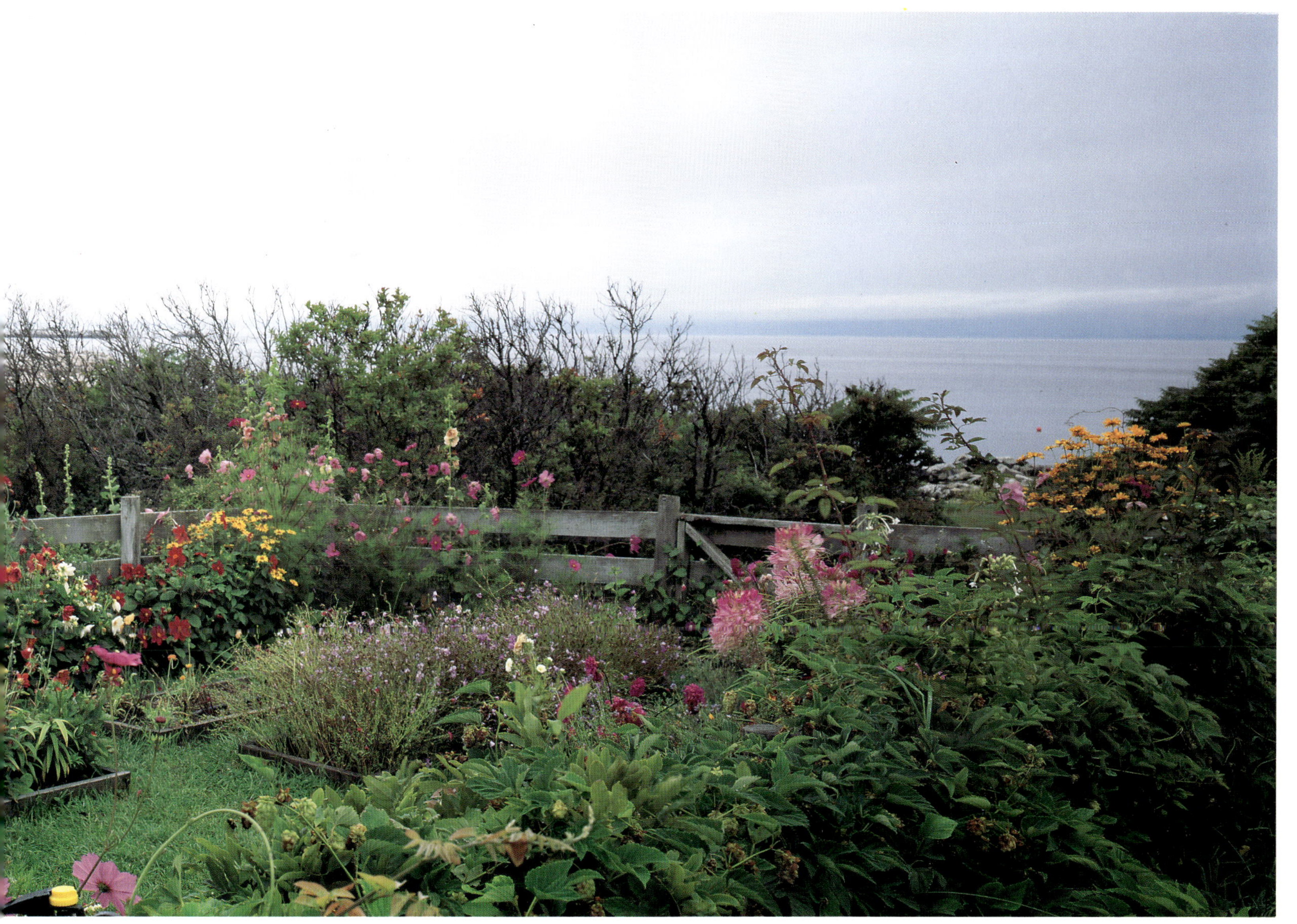

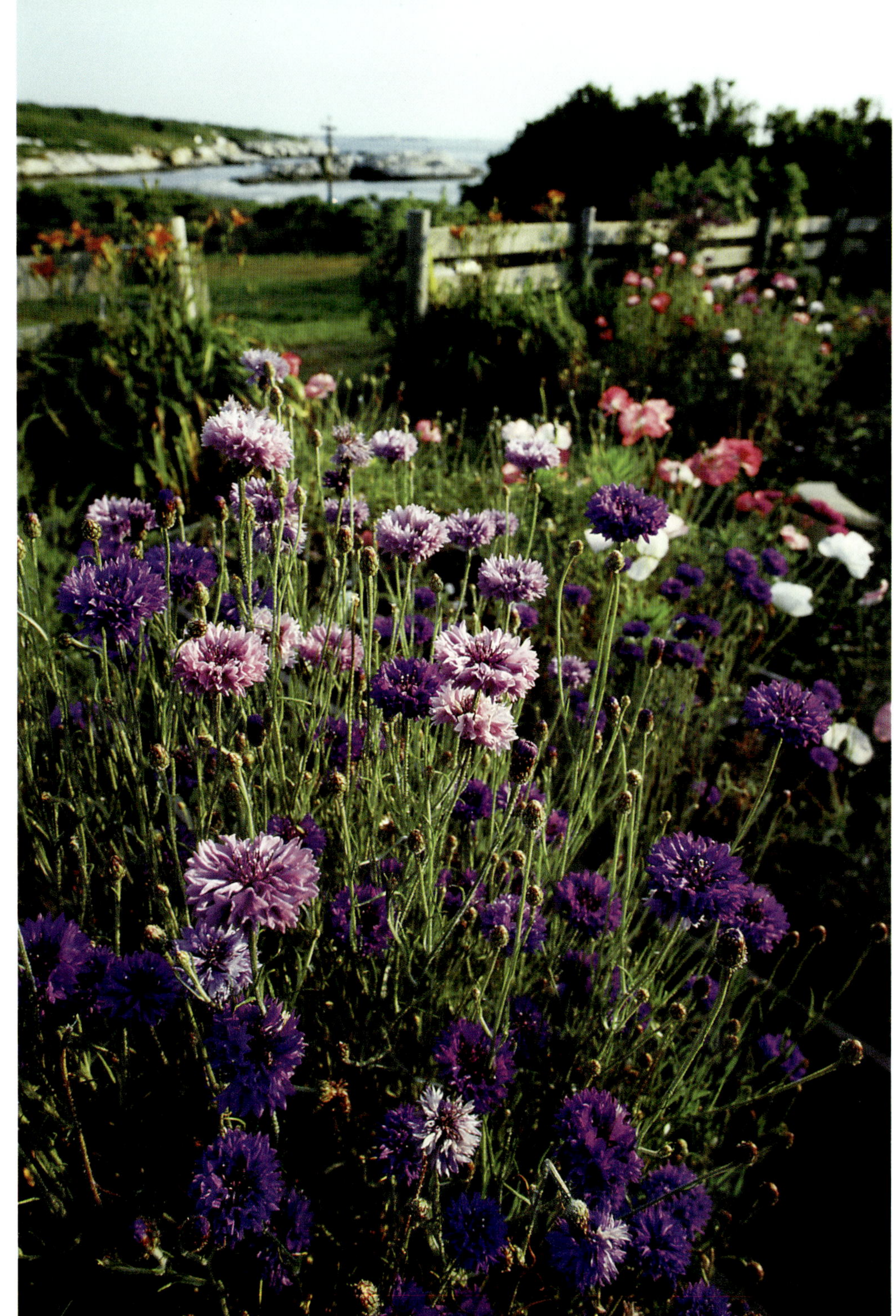

26 Celia's garden, Appledore.

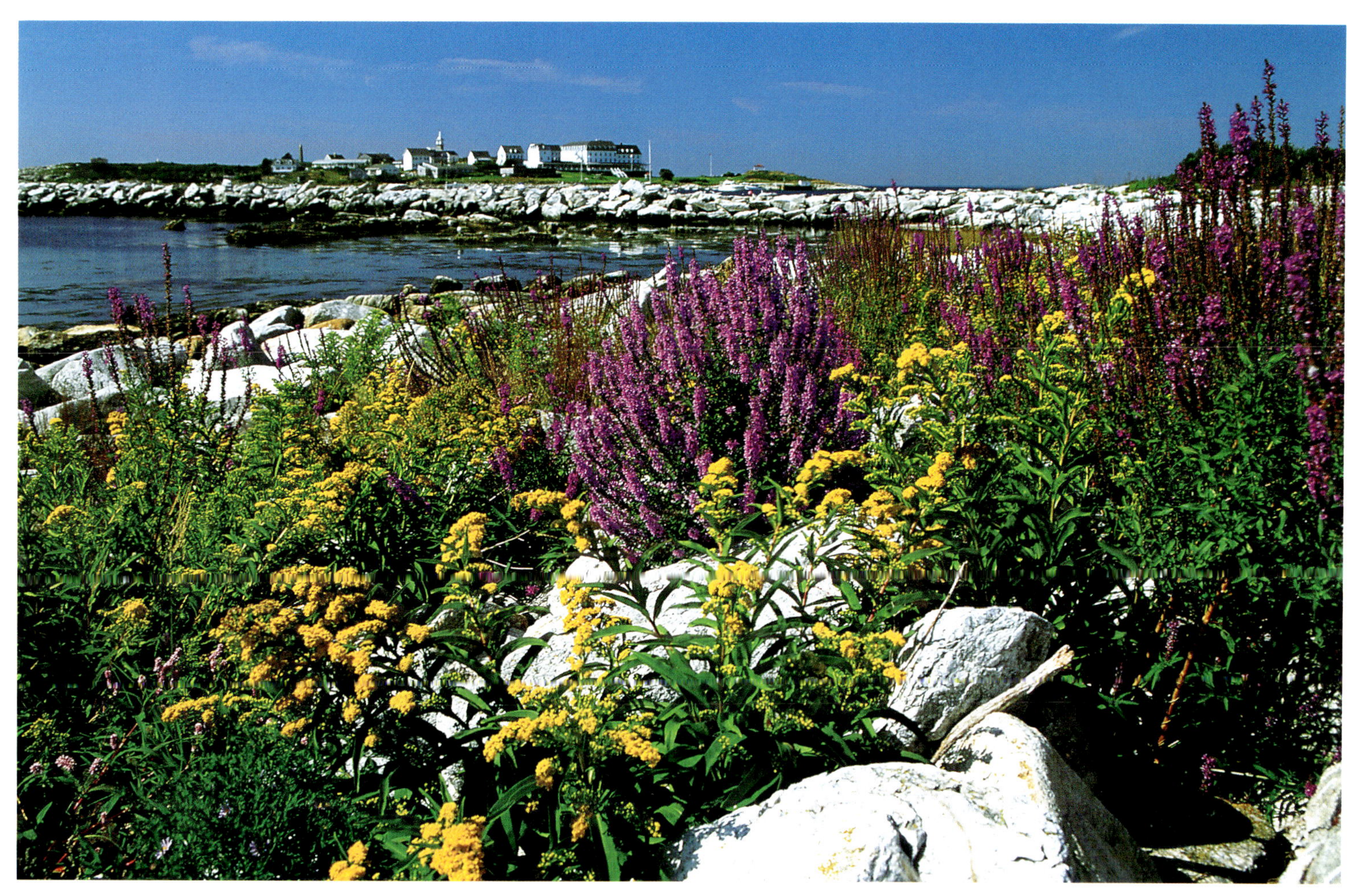

Wildflowers, Smuttynose.

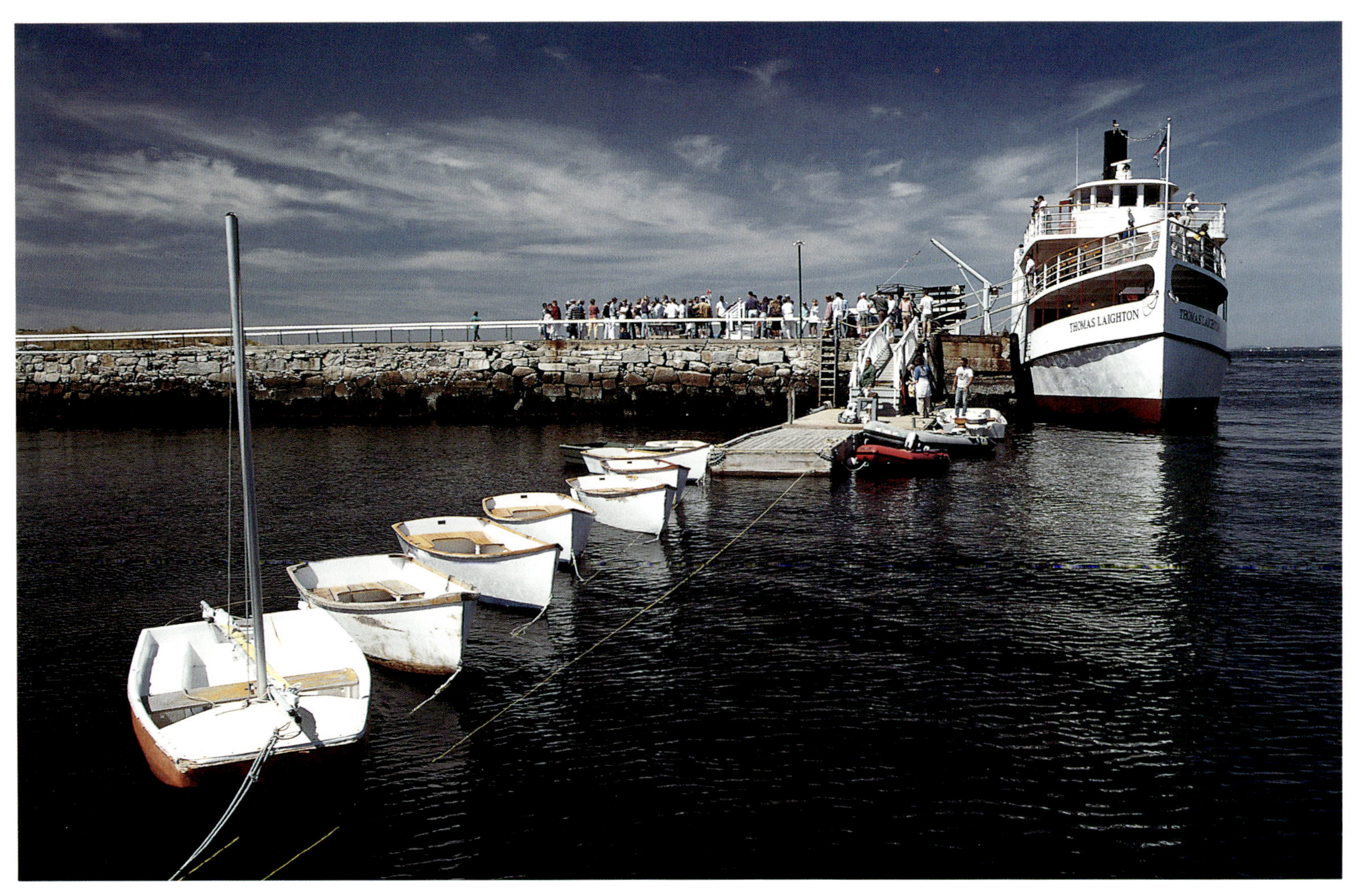

 Most people travel from Portsmouth to Star Island via the *Thomas Laighton*, the ferry named for Celia Thaxter's father.

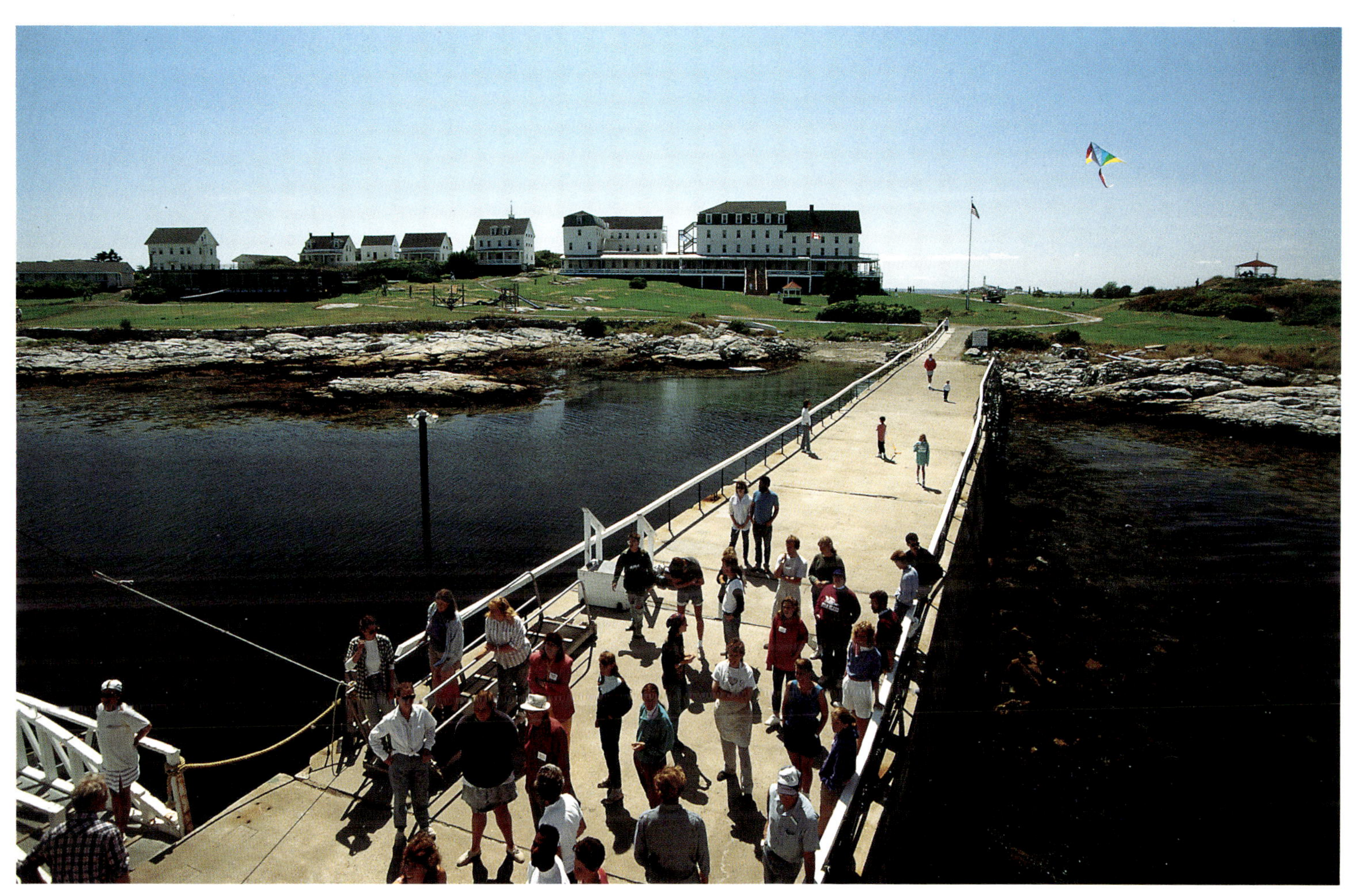

Star Island wharf, scene of cheerful welcomes and tearful goodbyes.

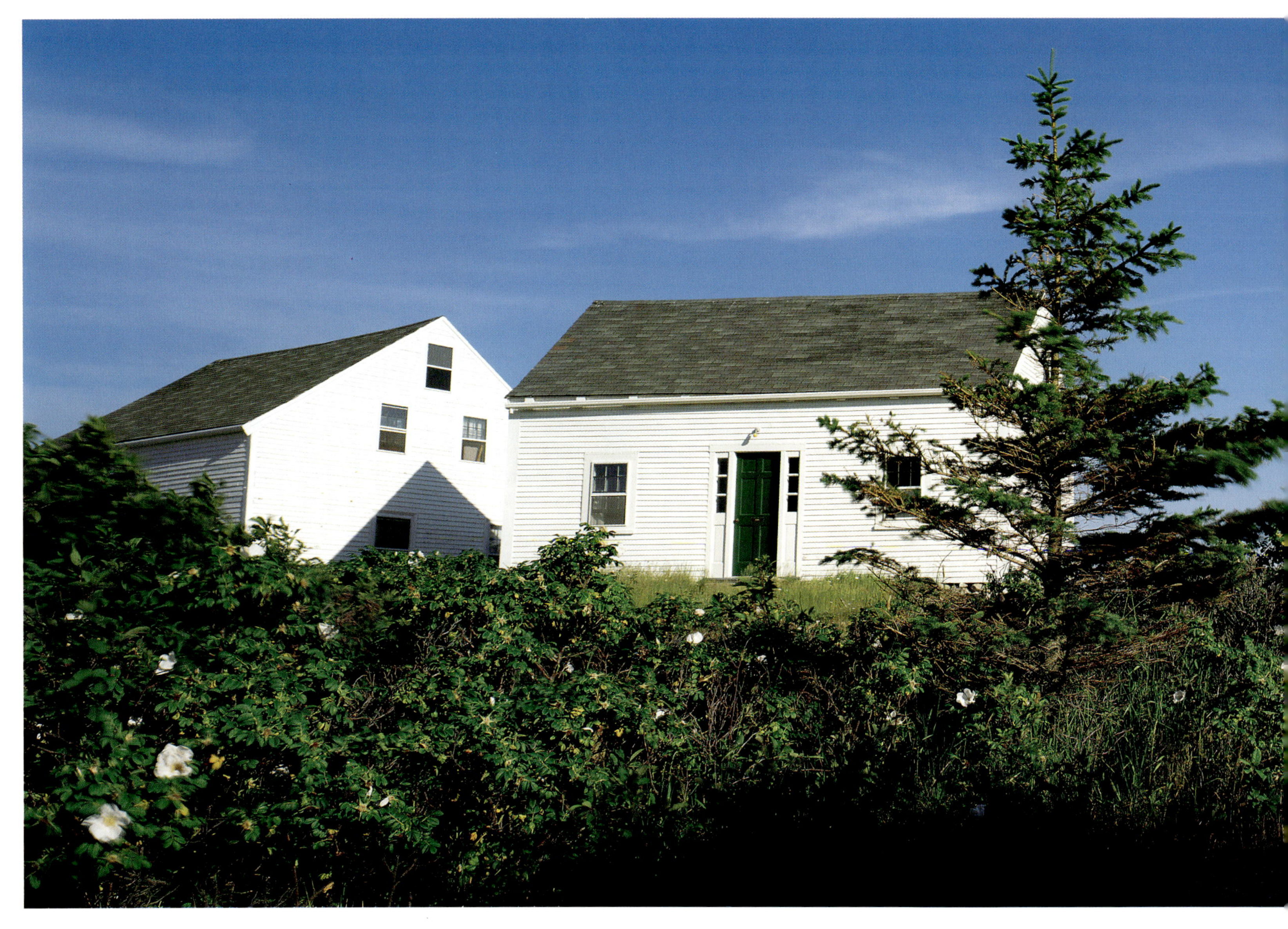

The two little Star Island cottages, built about 1780, are the oldest buildings on the islands. Gosport Church, circa 1800, is the spiritual center of the Shoals.

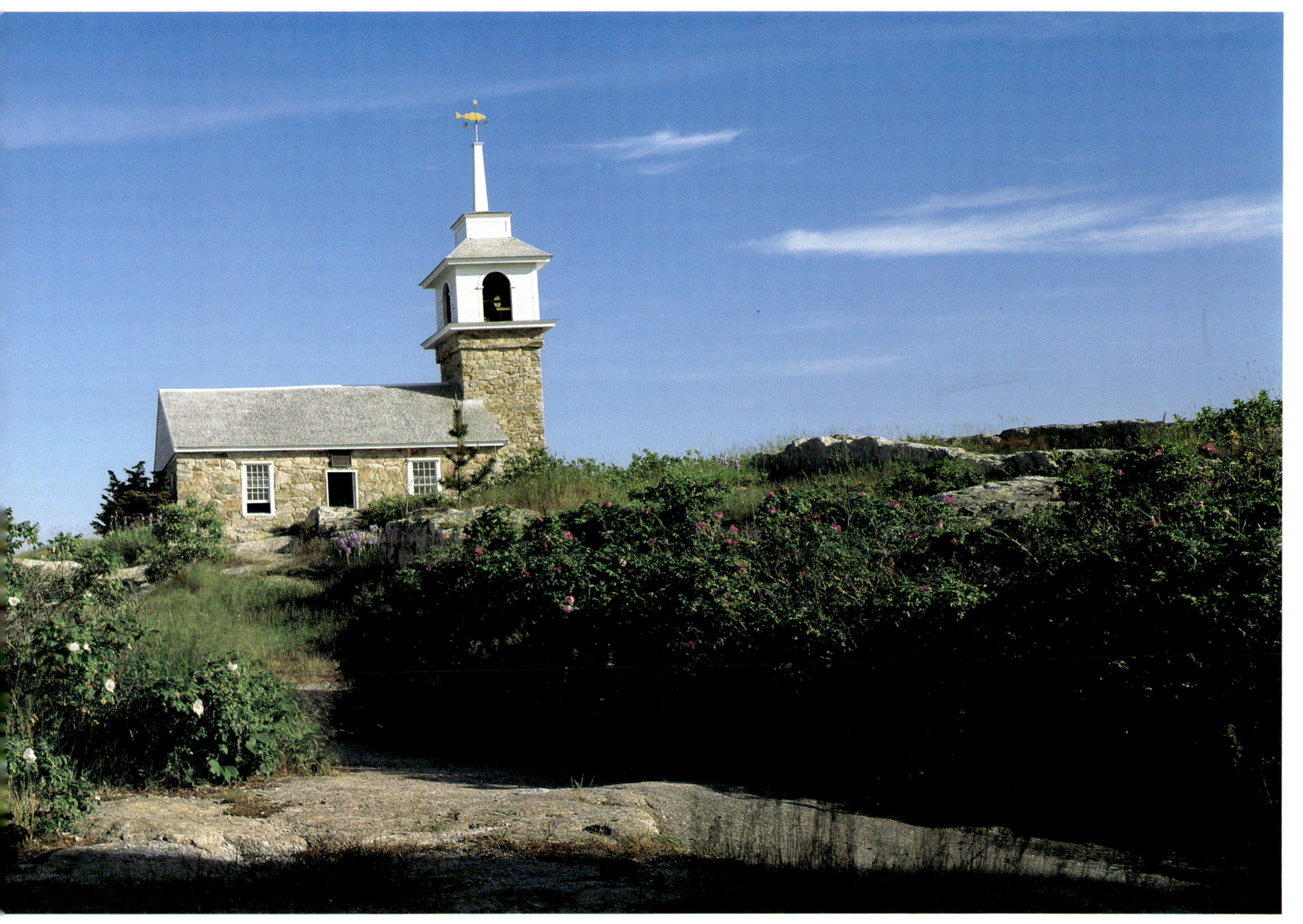

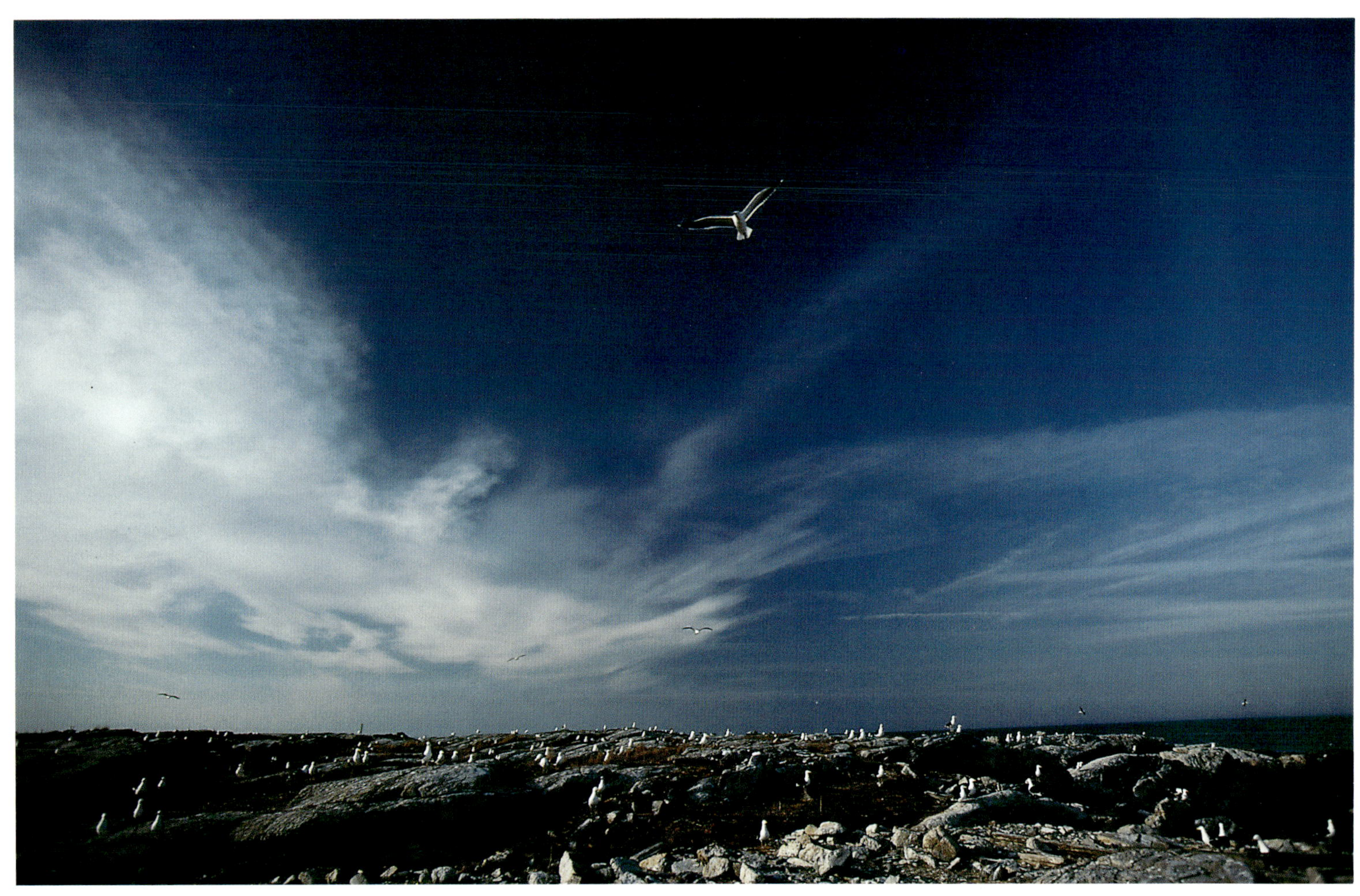

32 Great black-backed gull colony, Duck Island.

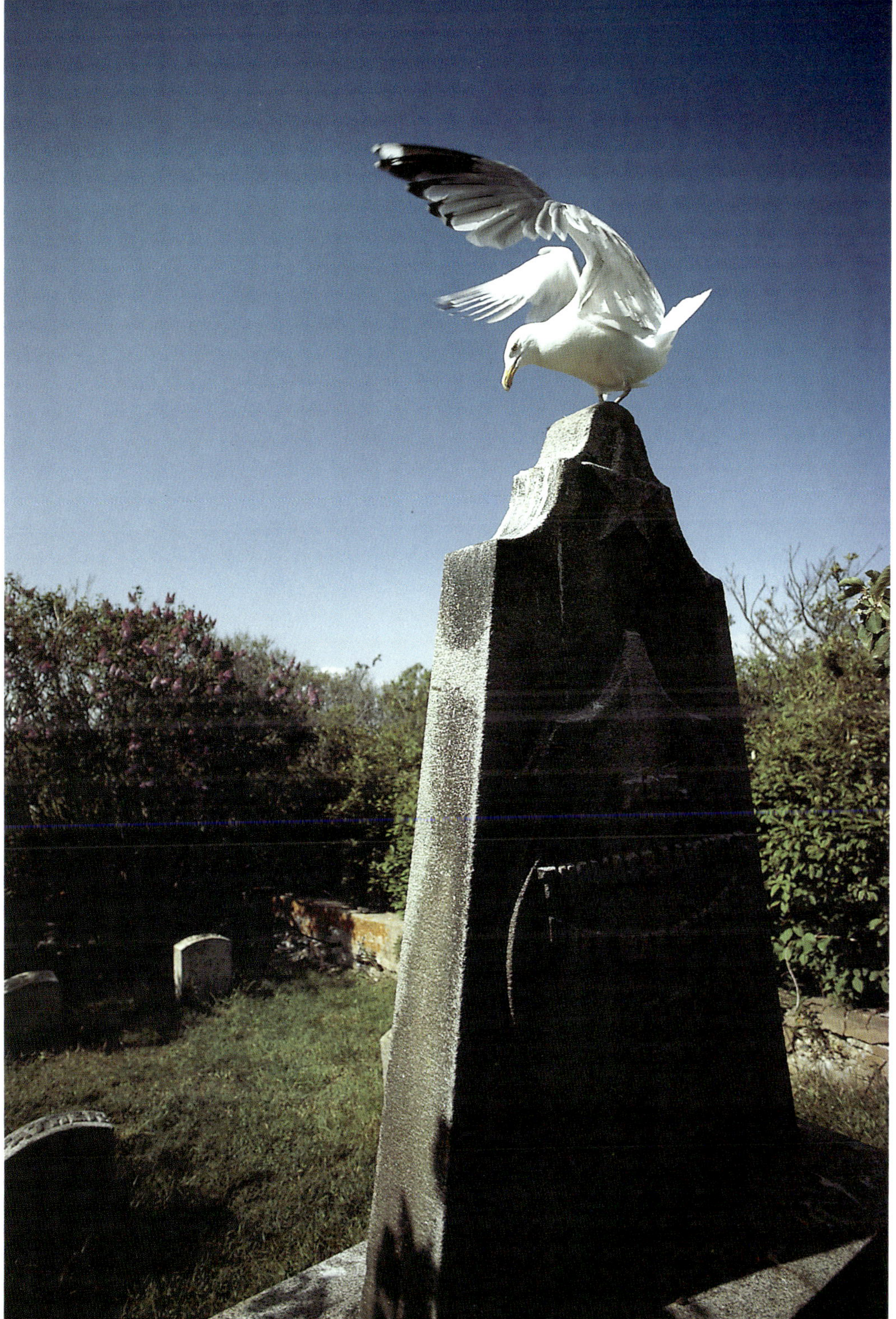

Laighton family cemetery, Appledore.

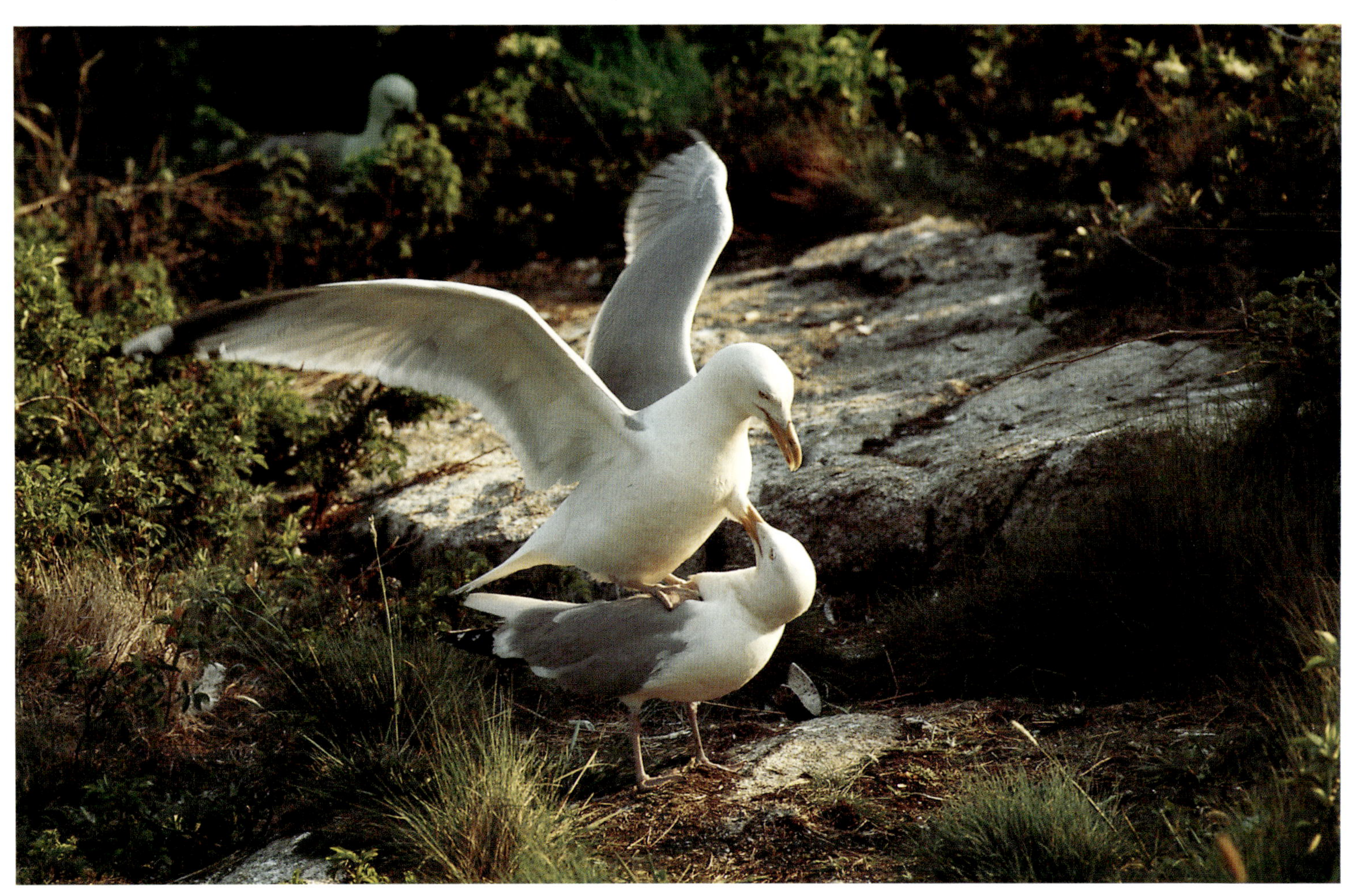

34 Herring gulls mating, Appledore.

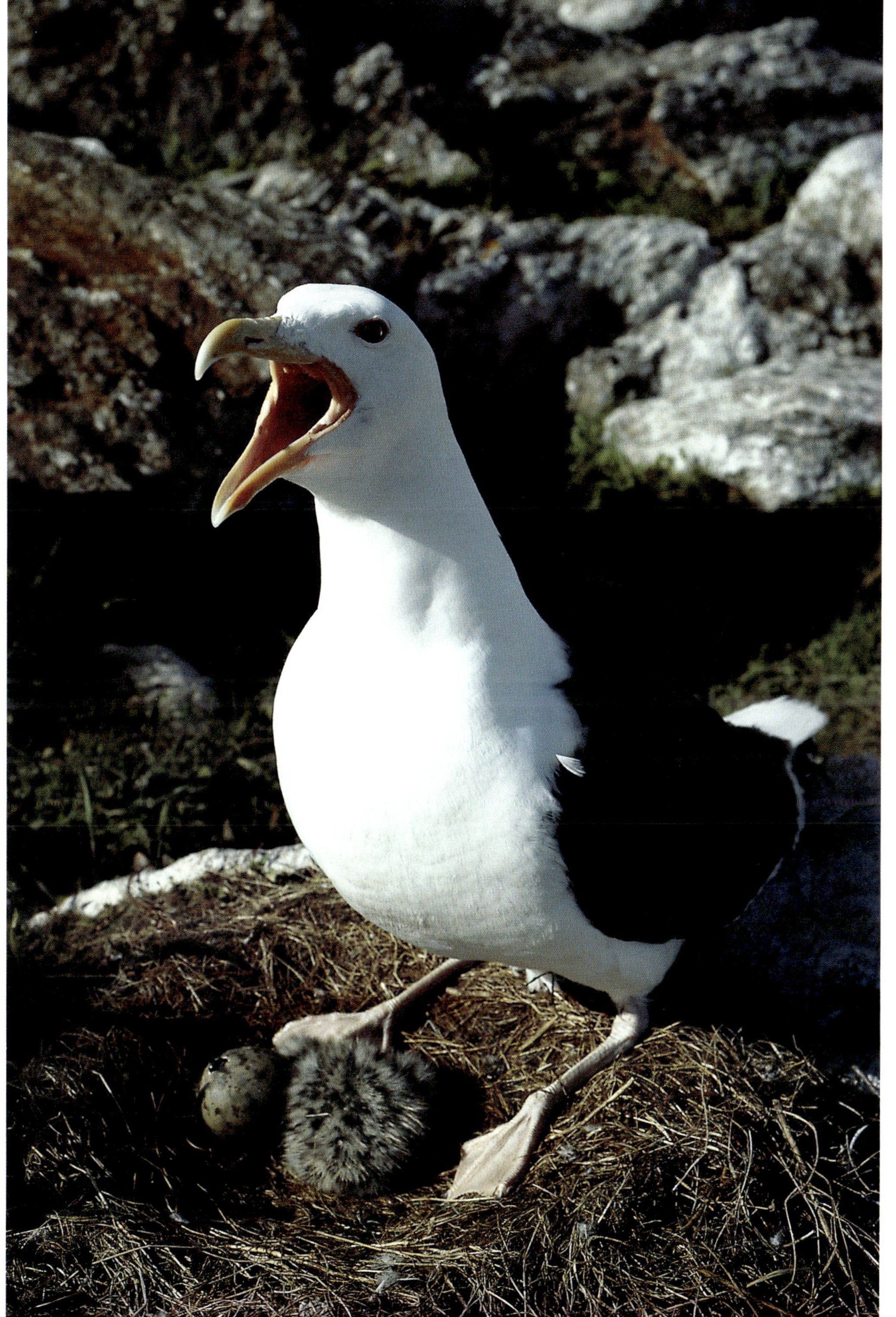

Great black-backed gull
at its nest, Appledore.

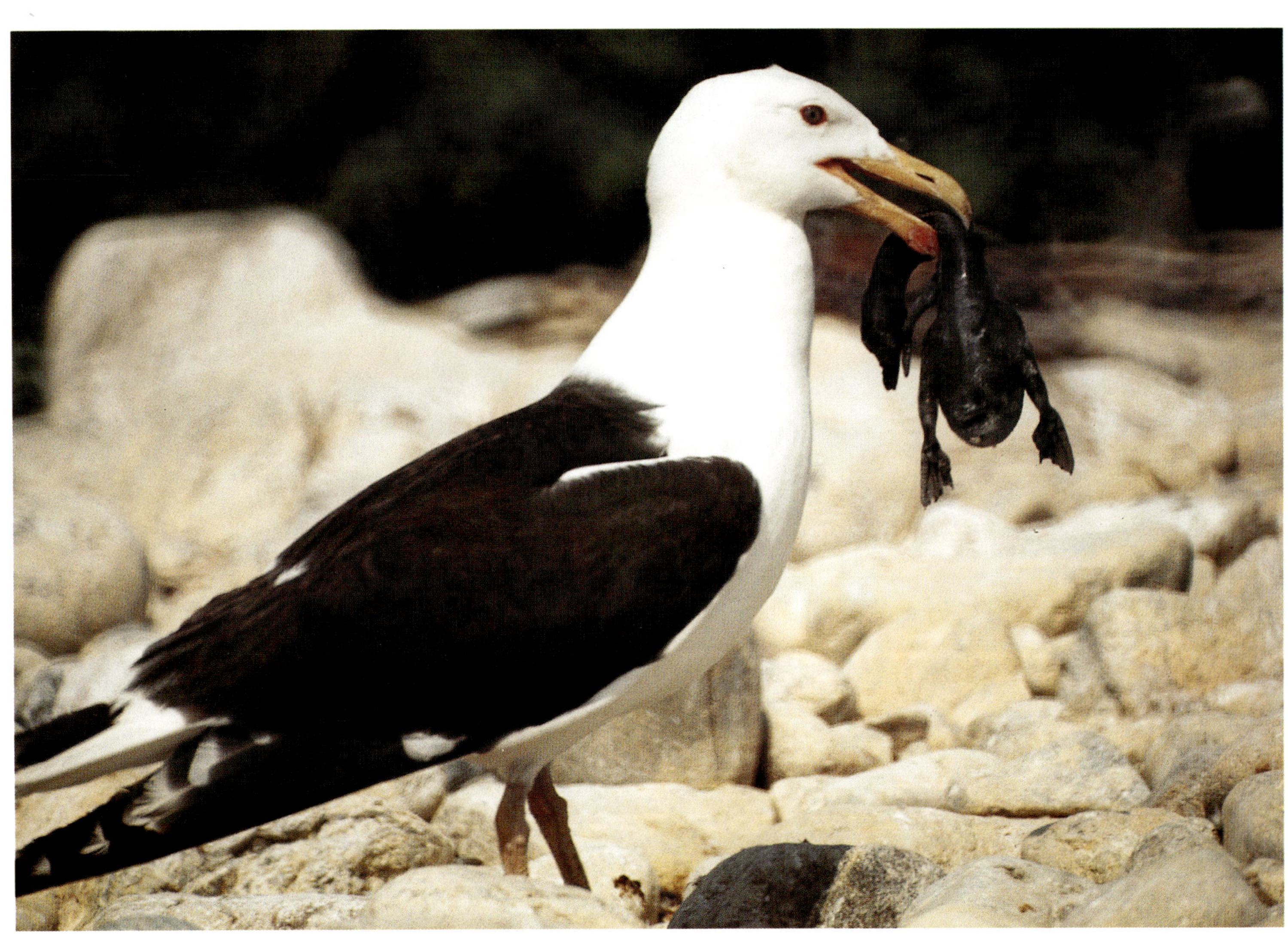

 Great black-backed gulls are quick to prey on the nests of cormorants (above) and herring gulls.

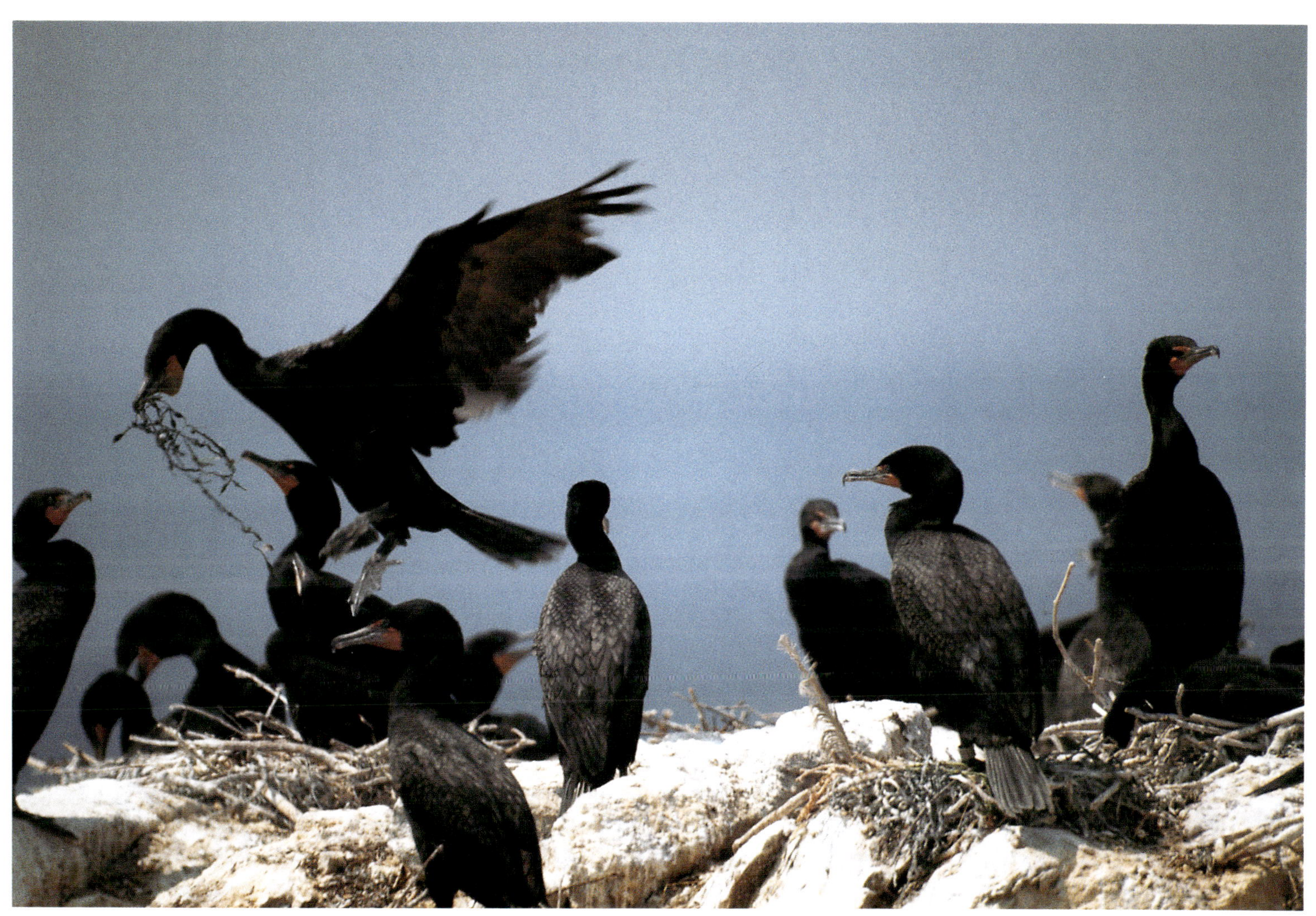

Double-crested cormants, Duck Island.

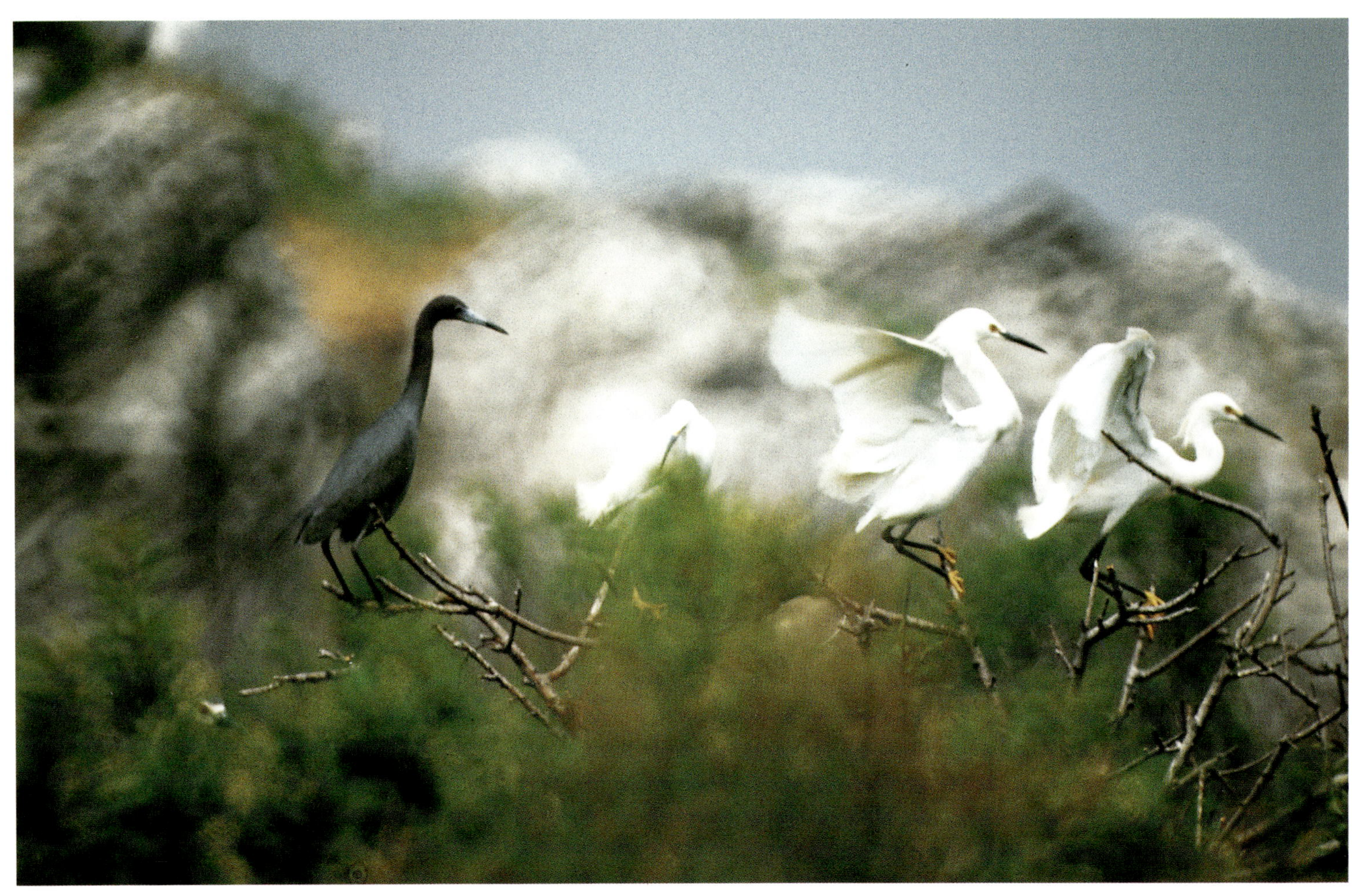

38 Little blue heron and snowy egrets, Appledore.

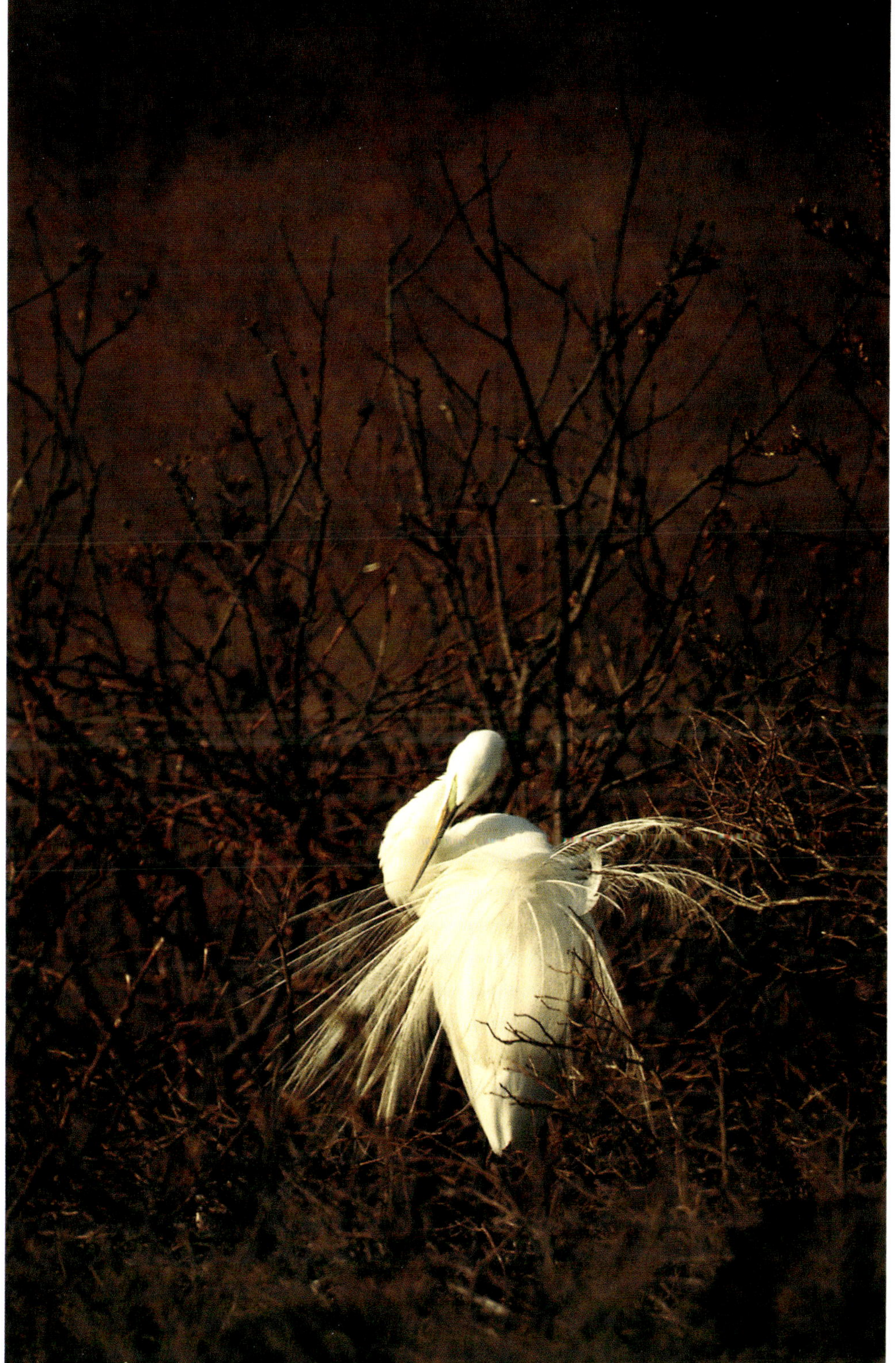

Common egret, Appledore.

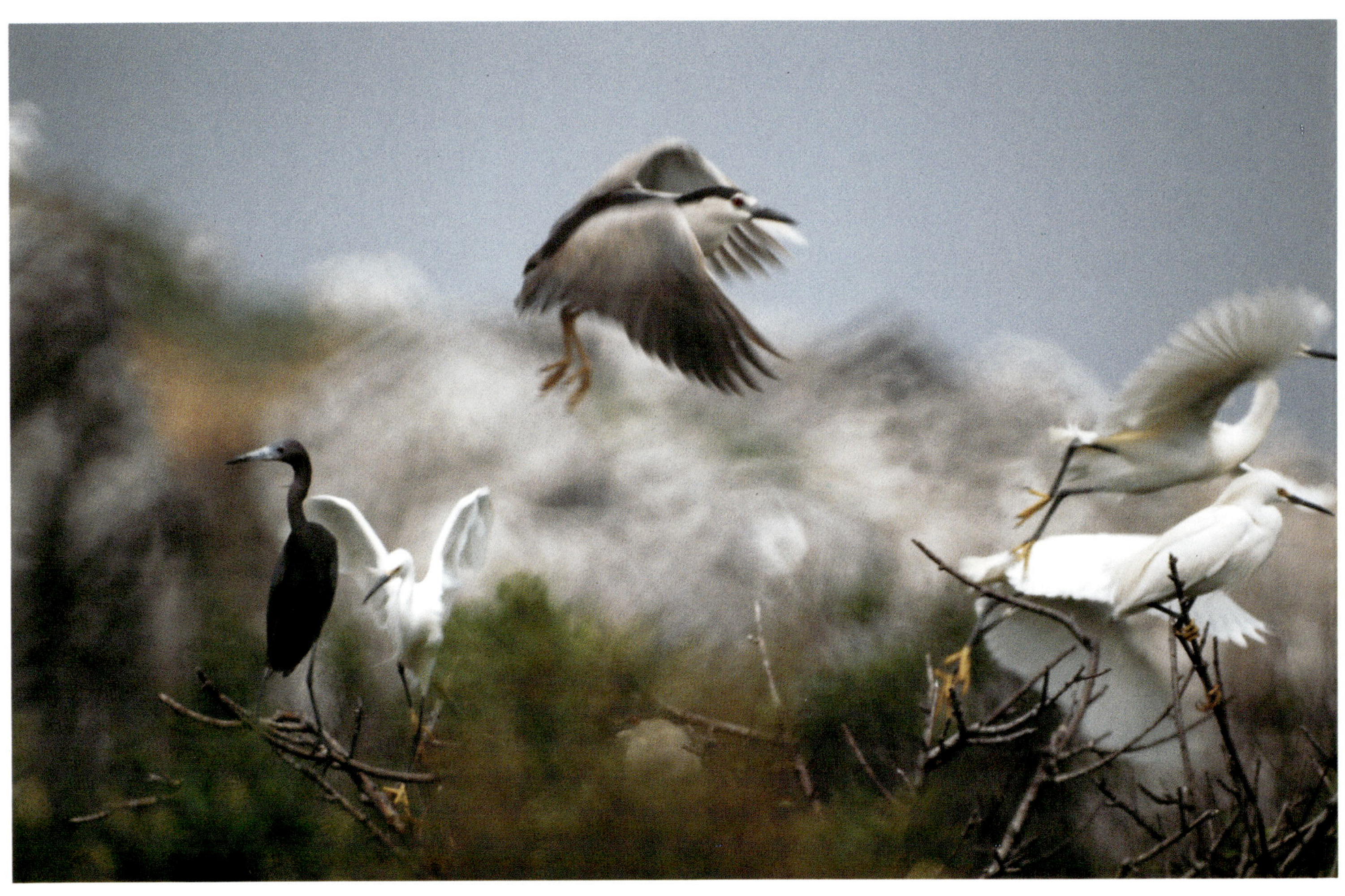

 Black-crowned night heron in flight, little blue heron, and snowy egrets, Appledore.

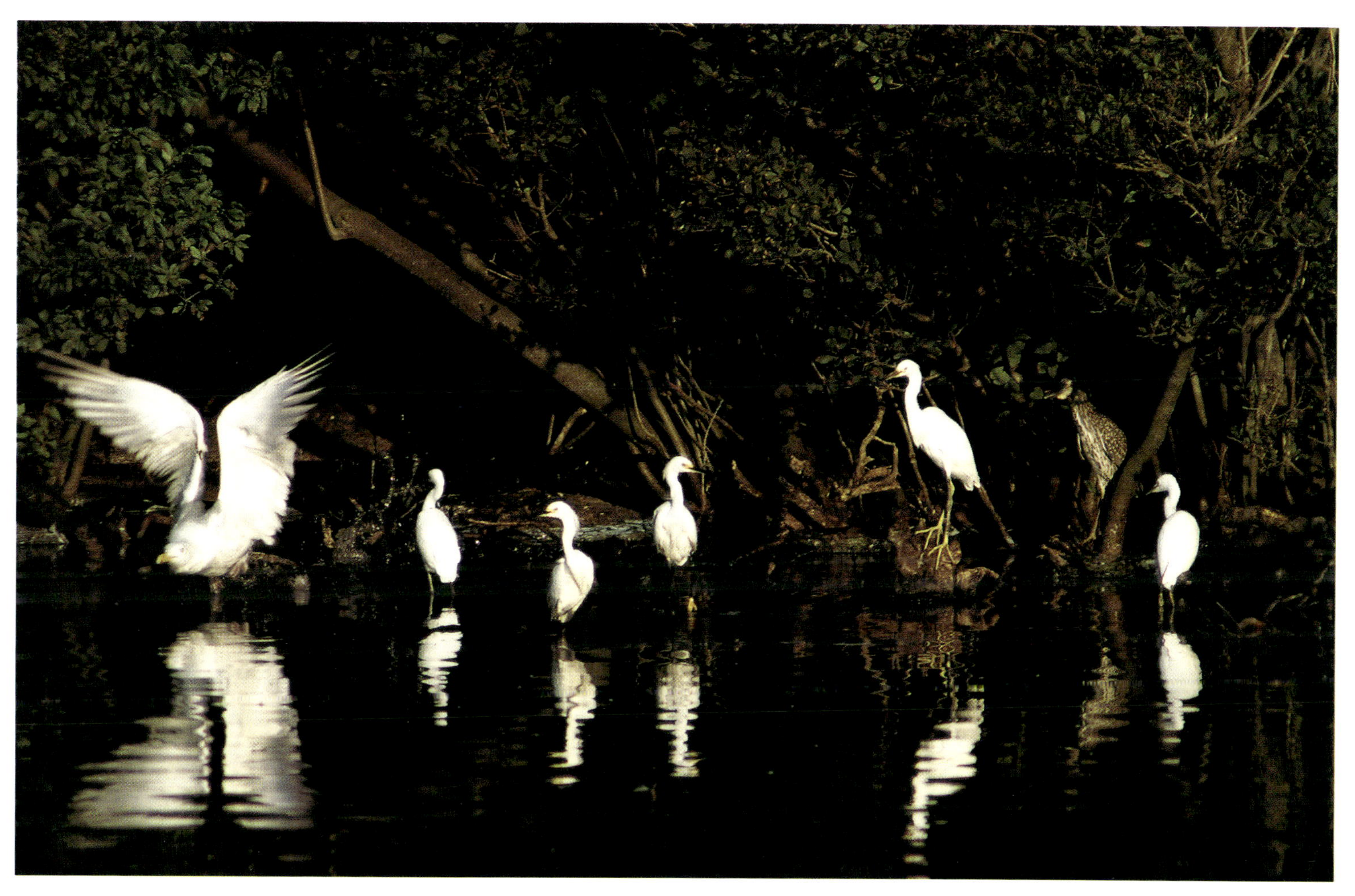

Herring gull in flight, with snowy egrets, and an immature black-crowned night heron at right, Crystal Lake, Appledore.

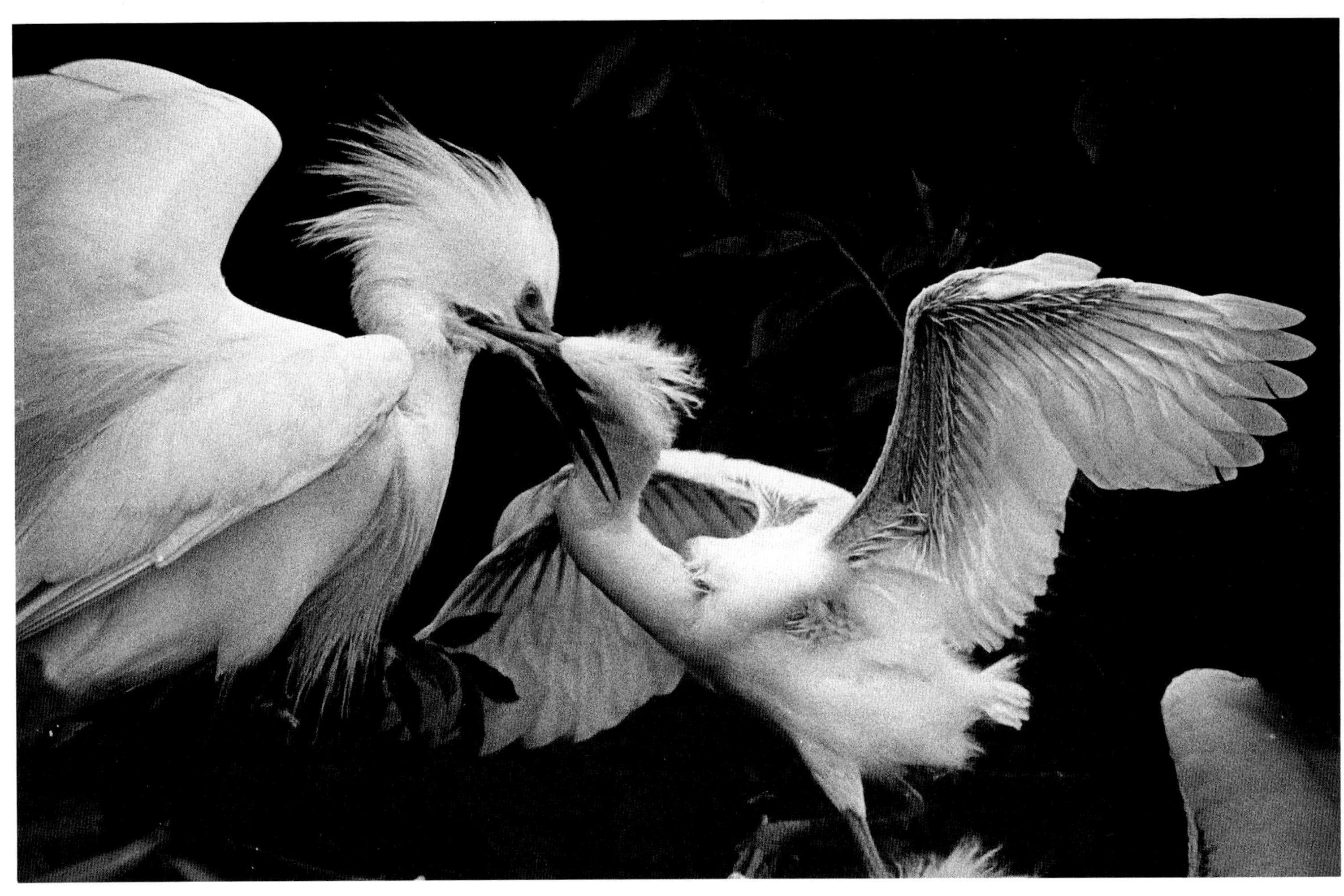

 Snowy egret feeding its young.

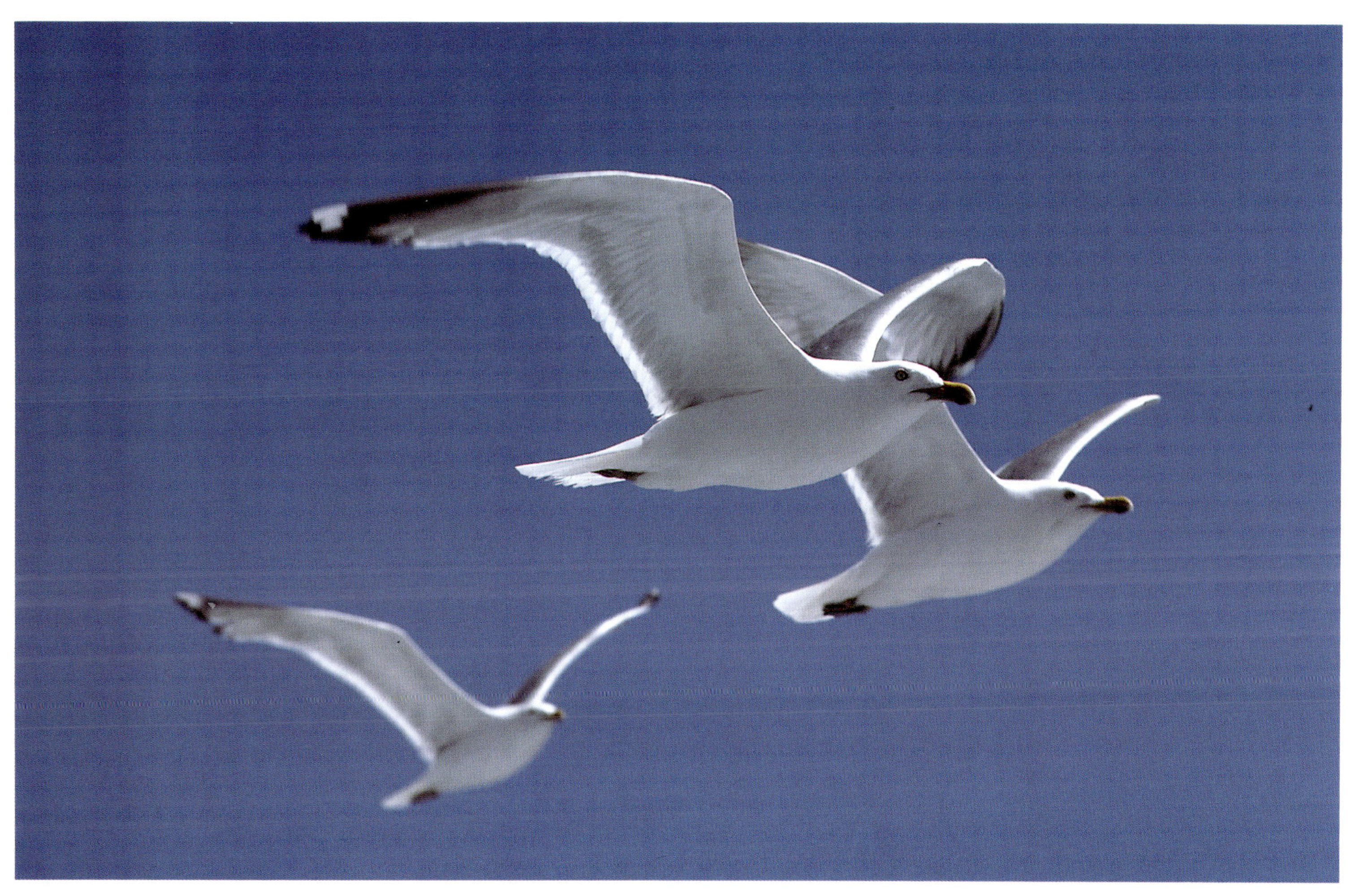

Herring gulls, off Appledore.

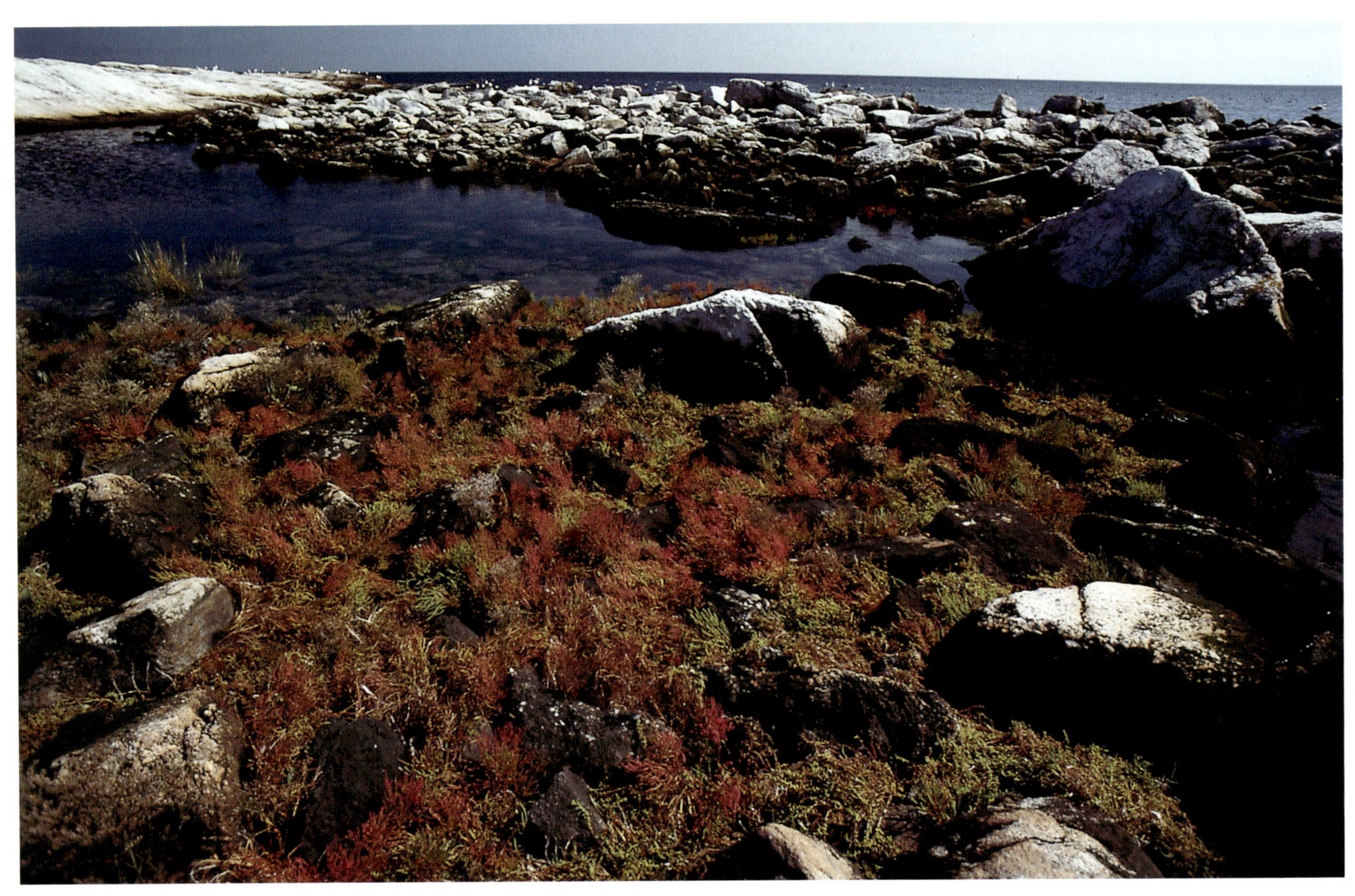

 Glasswort (Salicornia) colors an autumn tidepool, Smuttynose.

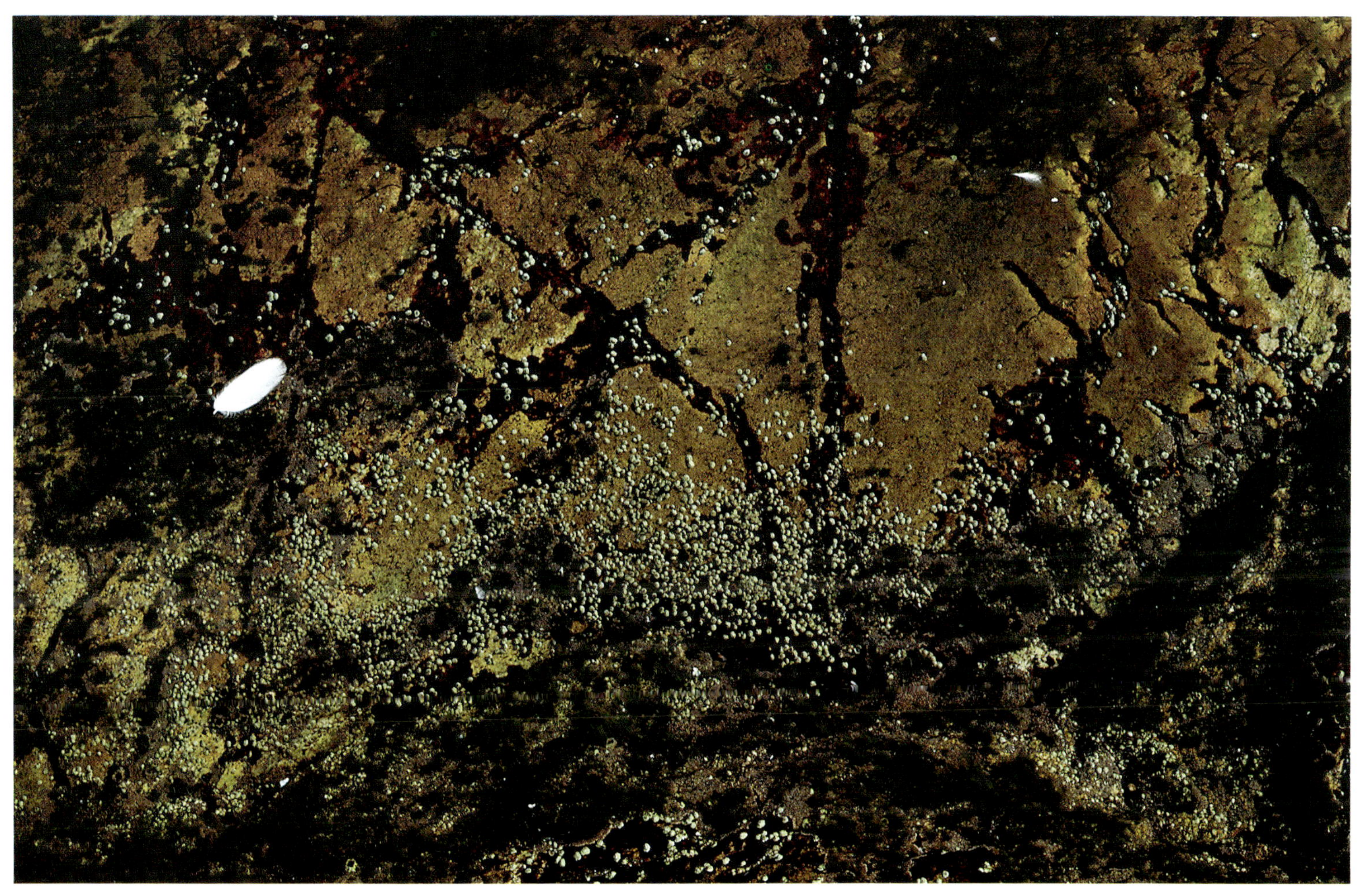

A gull feather floats on a shallow tidepool, Appledore.

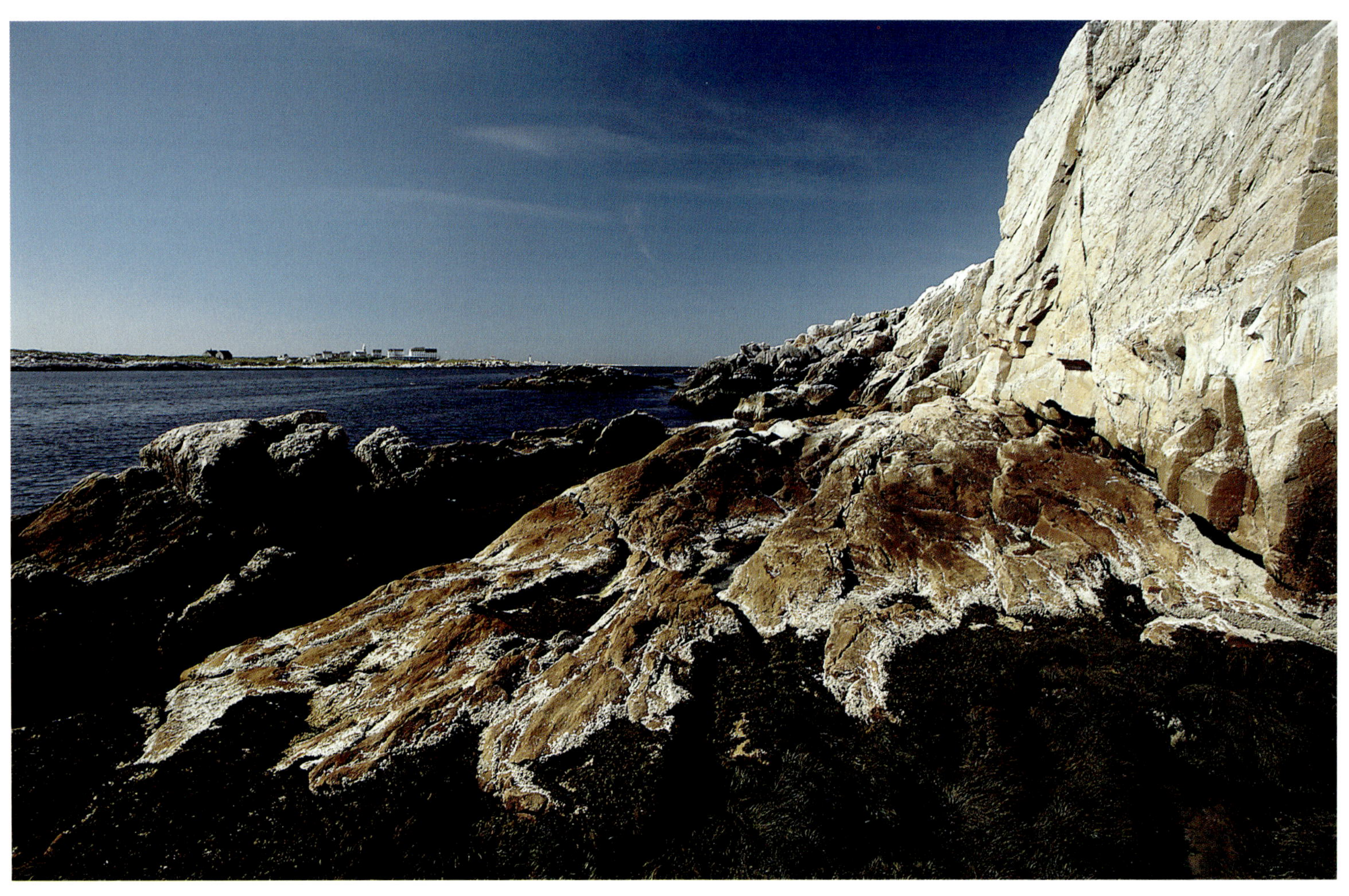

46 The barnacle zone, Appledore.

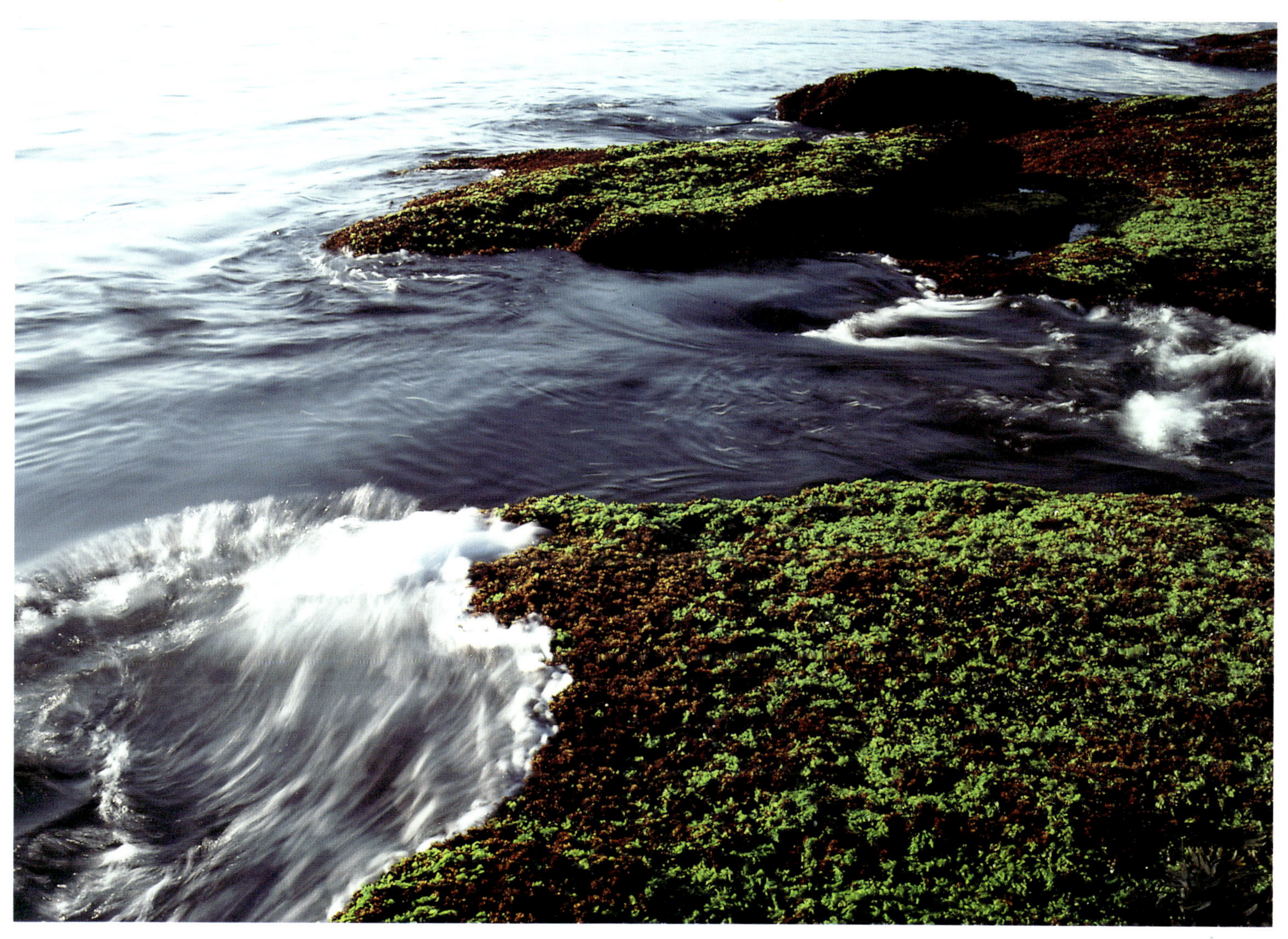

Sea lettuce, intertidal zone, Star Island.

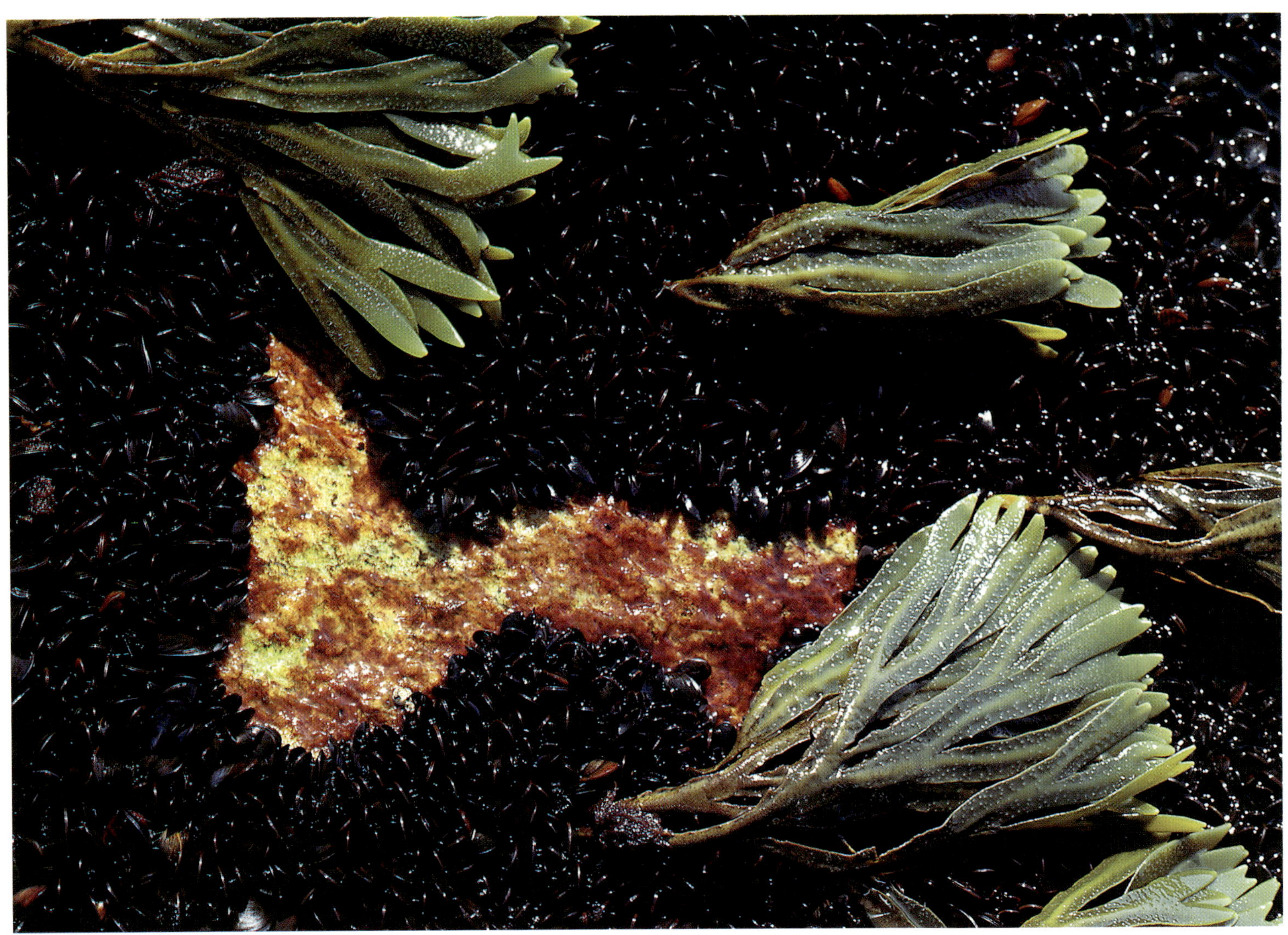

48 Low tide zone, Appledore.

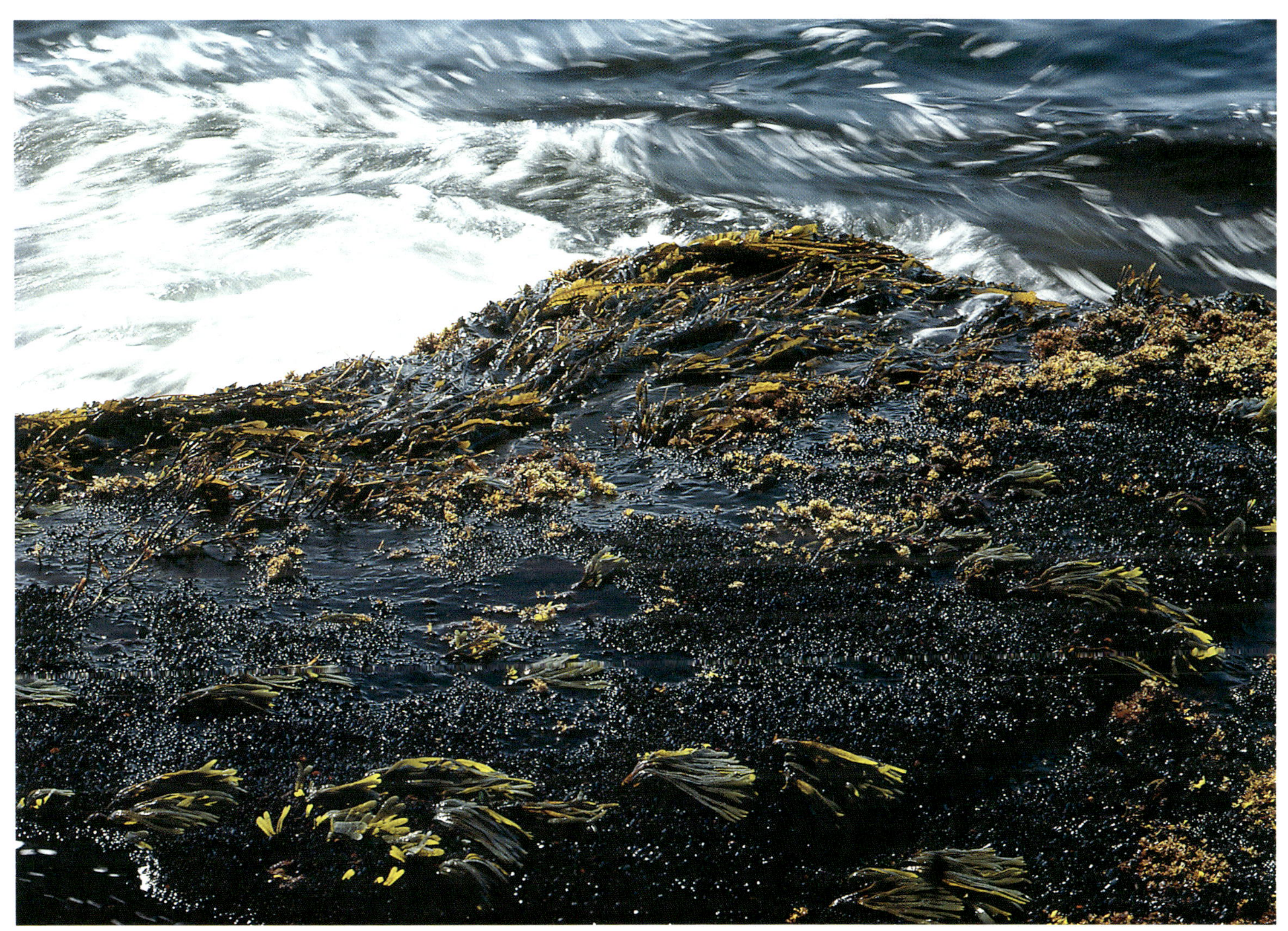

Marine algae covers intertidal rocks like a blanket, Appledore.

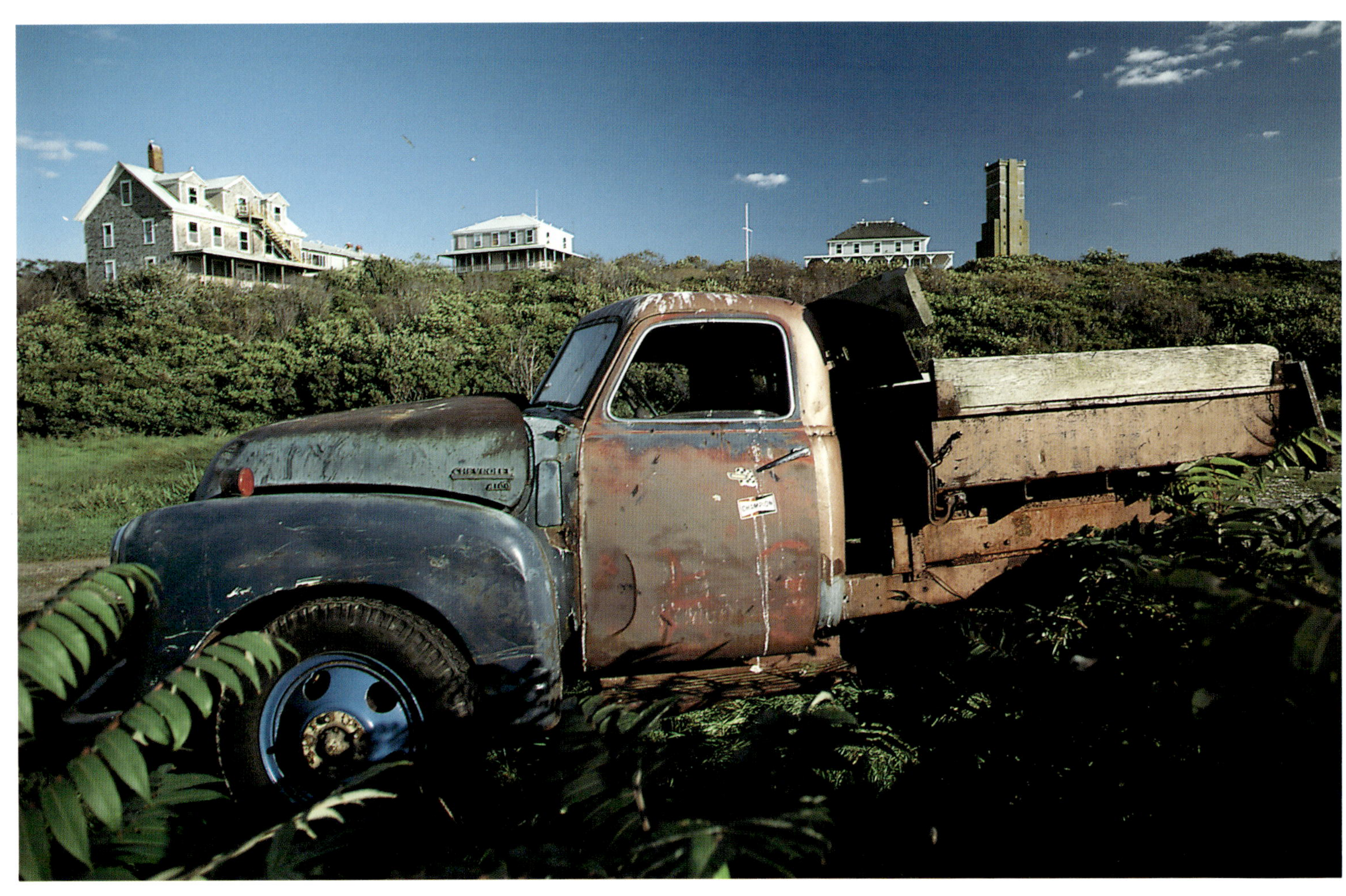

 "Old Joe," faithful truck of the Shoals Marine Laboratory, in retirement, Appledore.

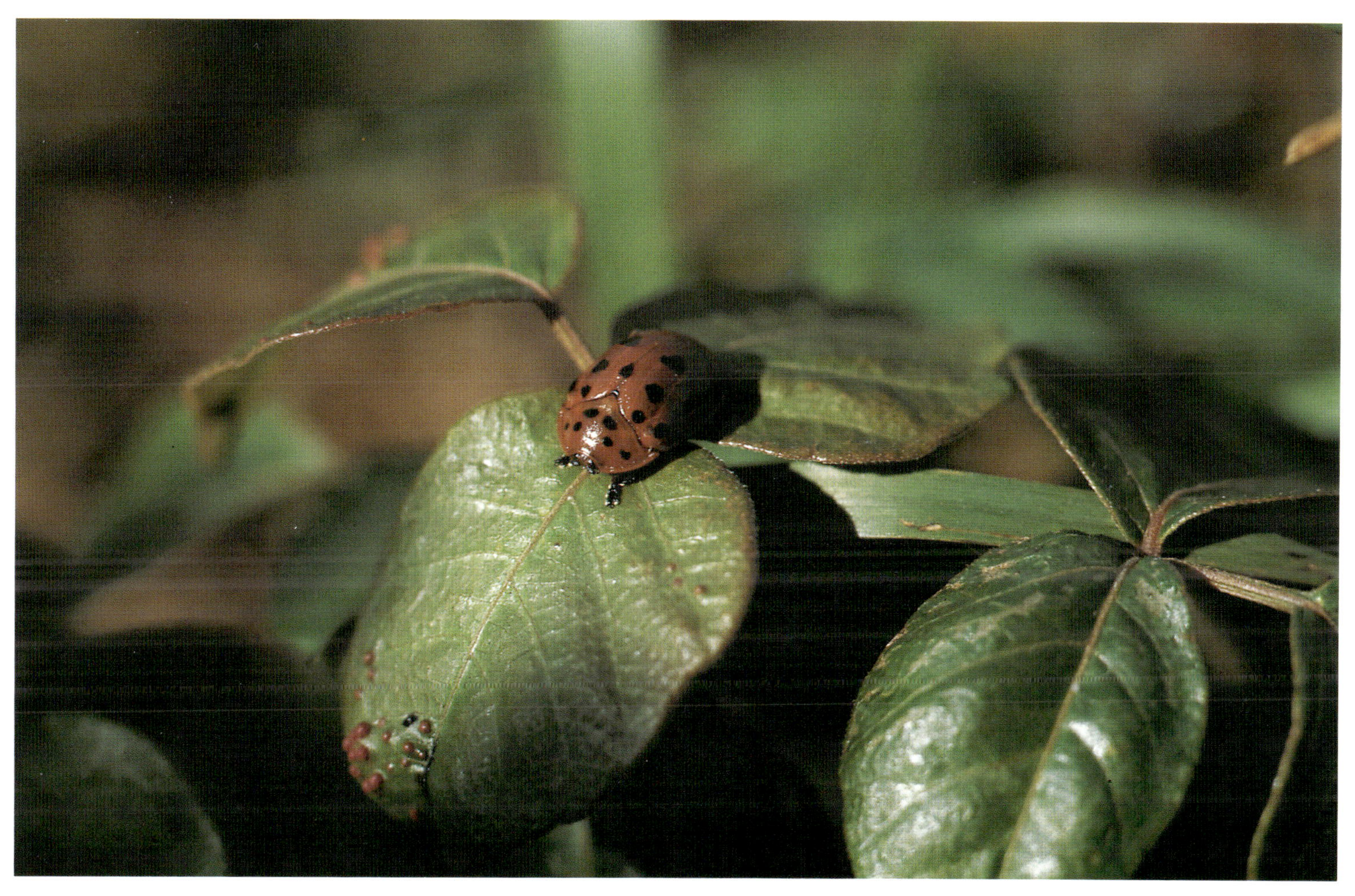

Lady bug on poison ivy. The itch-causing plant grows as a lush blanket on many parts of the islands and reaches heights over six feet on Appledore.

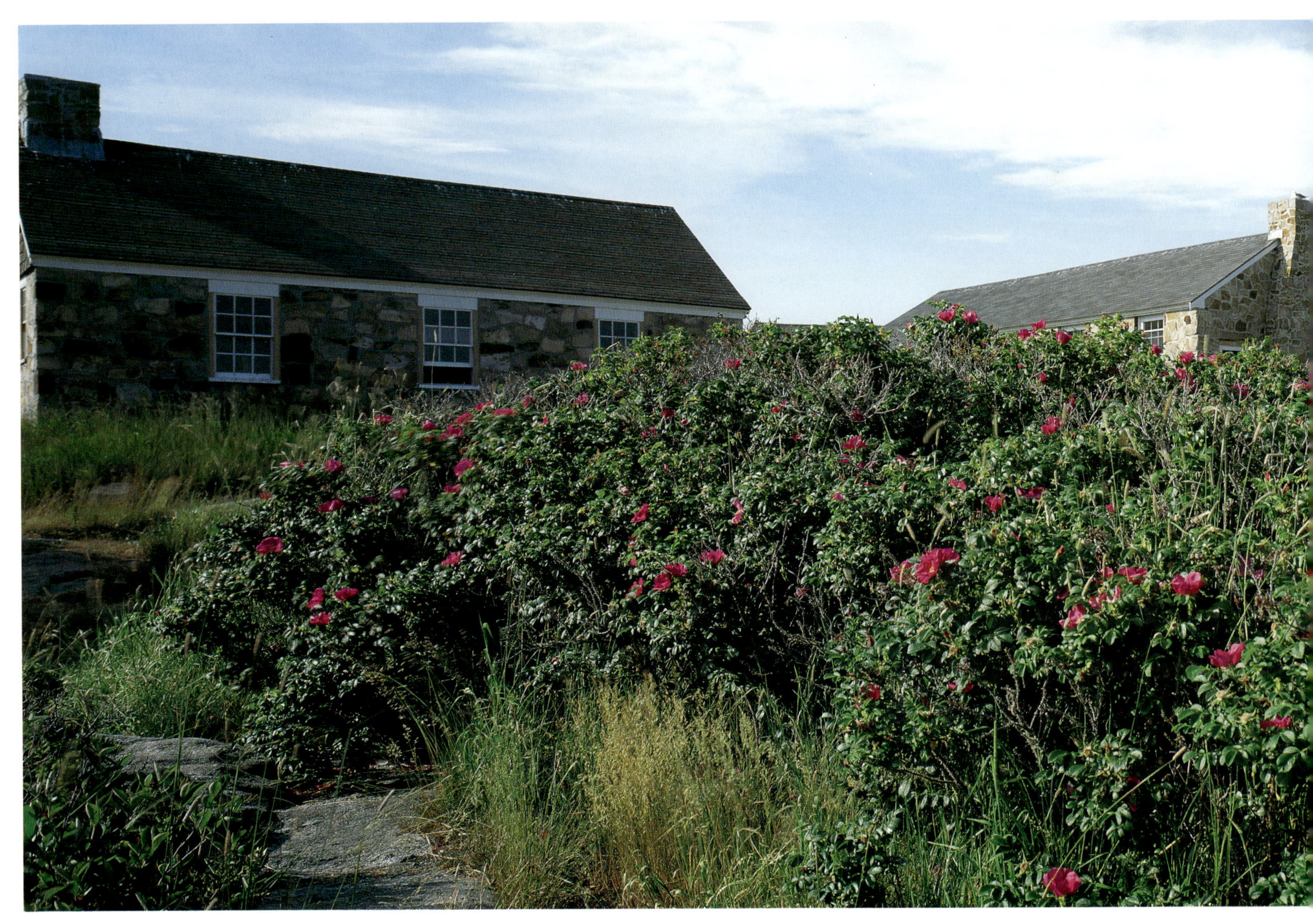

 Late afternoon, Star Island. Stone buildings were constructed in this century by the Star Island Conference Center.

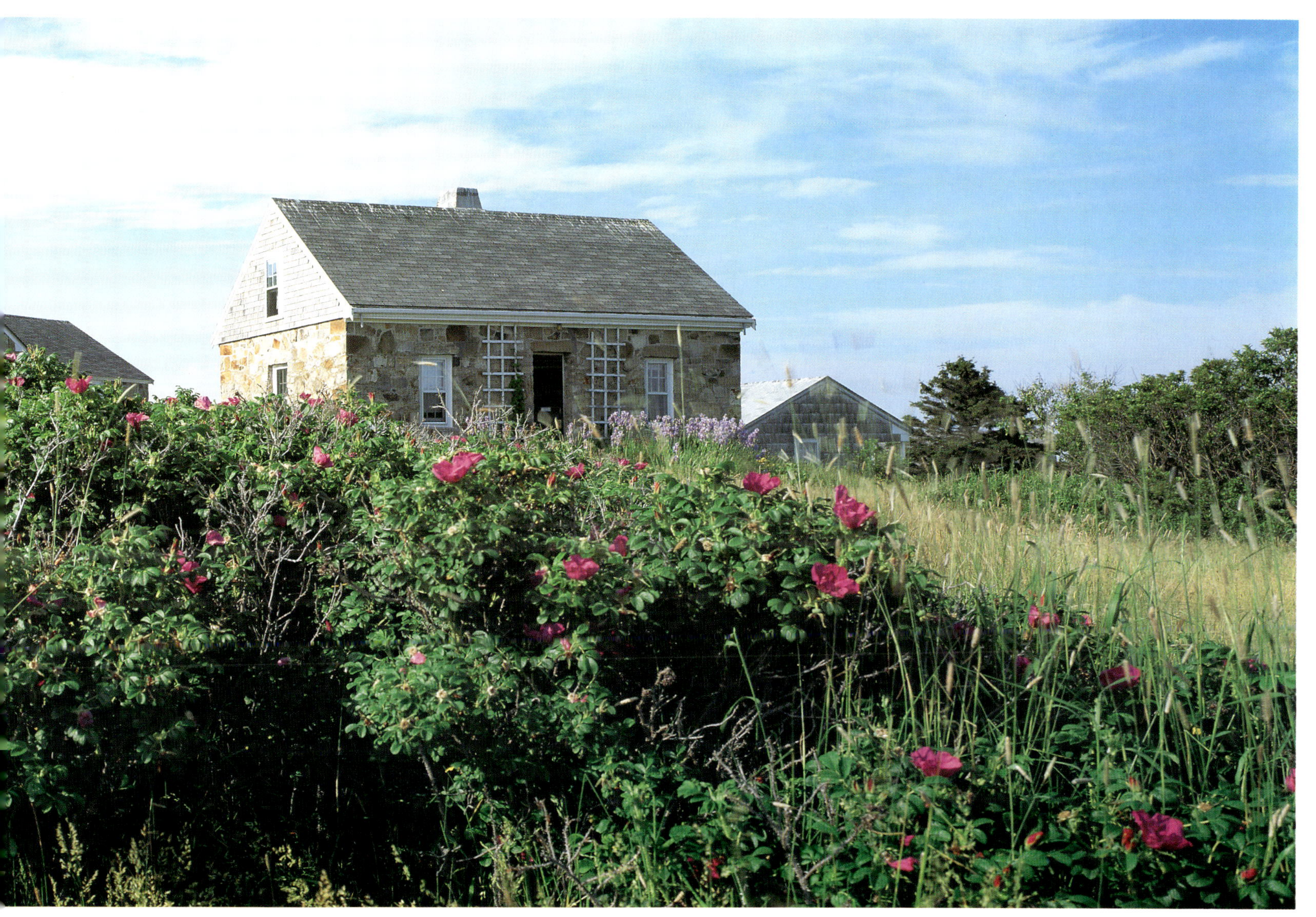

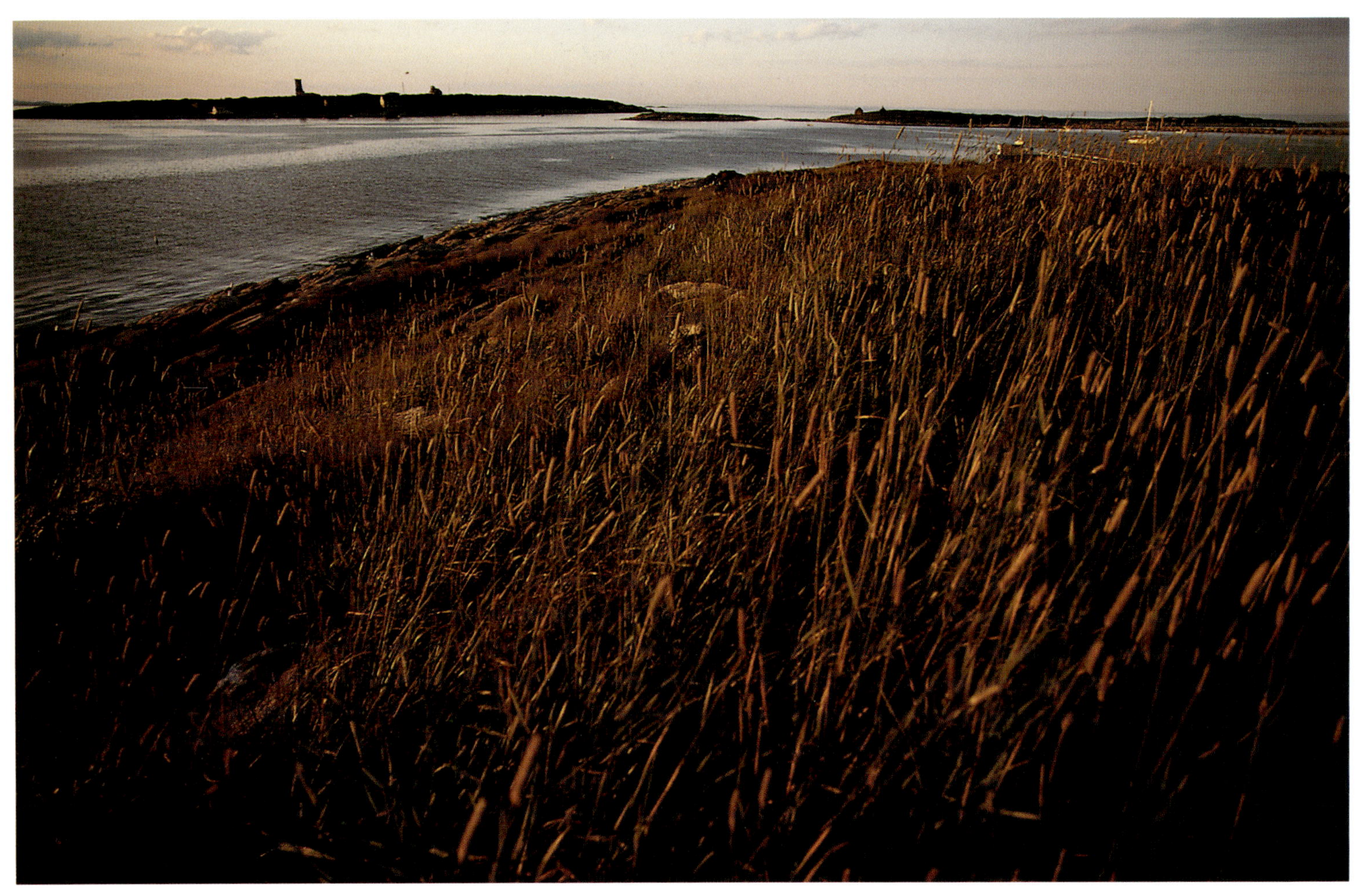

54 Late afternoon, Star Island.

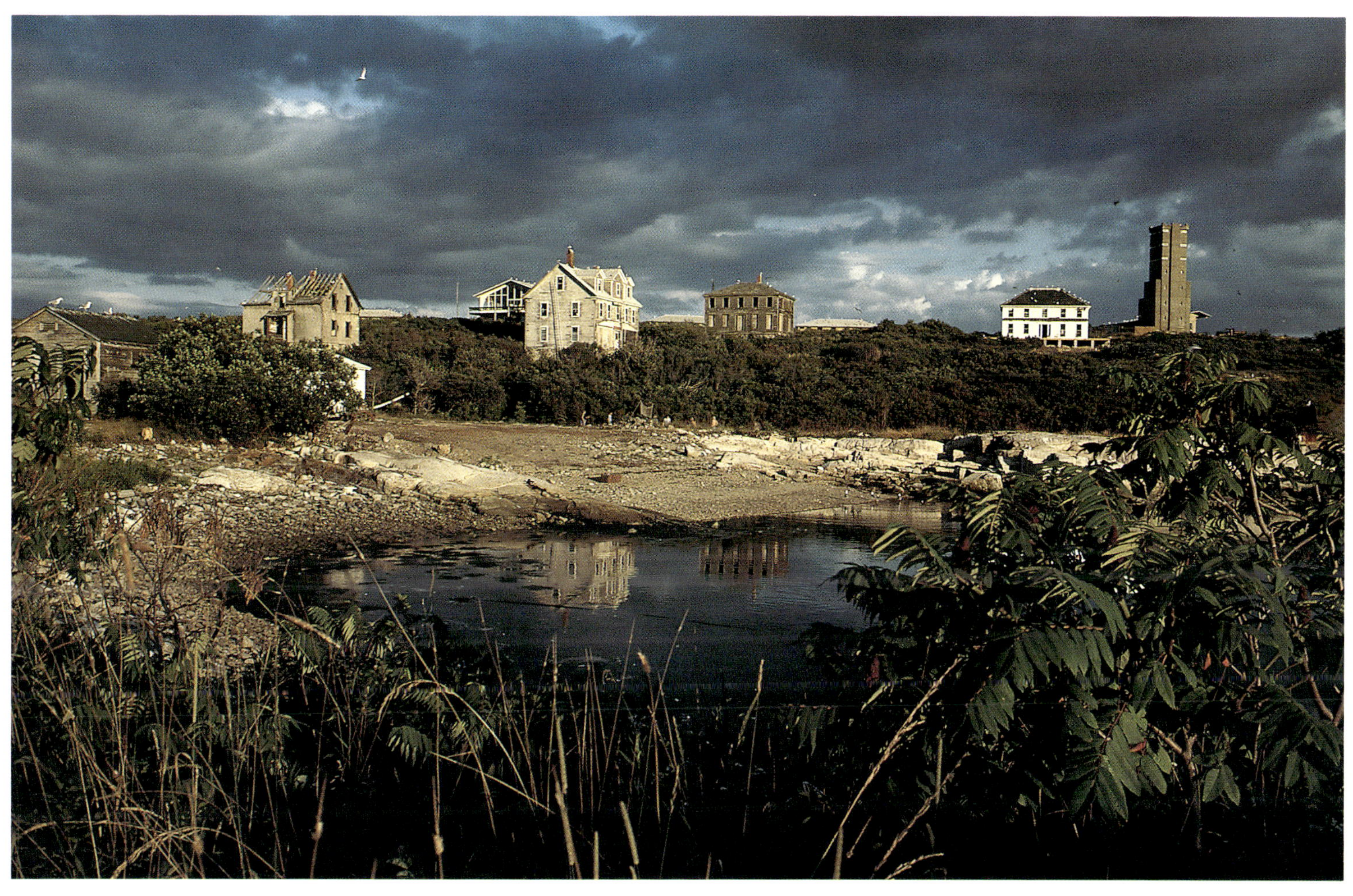

After the storm, Appledore. Large private house at left is gone, the two buildings at center have been restored, joining the other buildings shown as part of the Shoals Marine Laboratory.

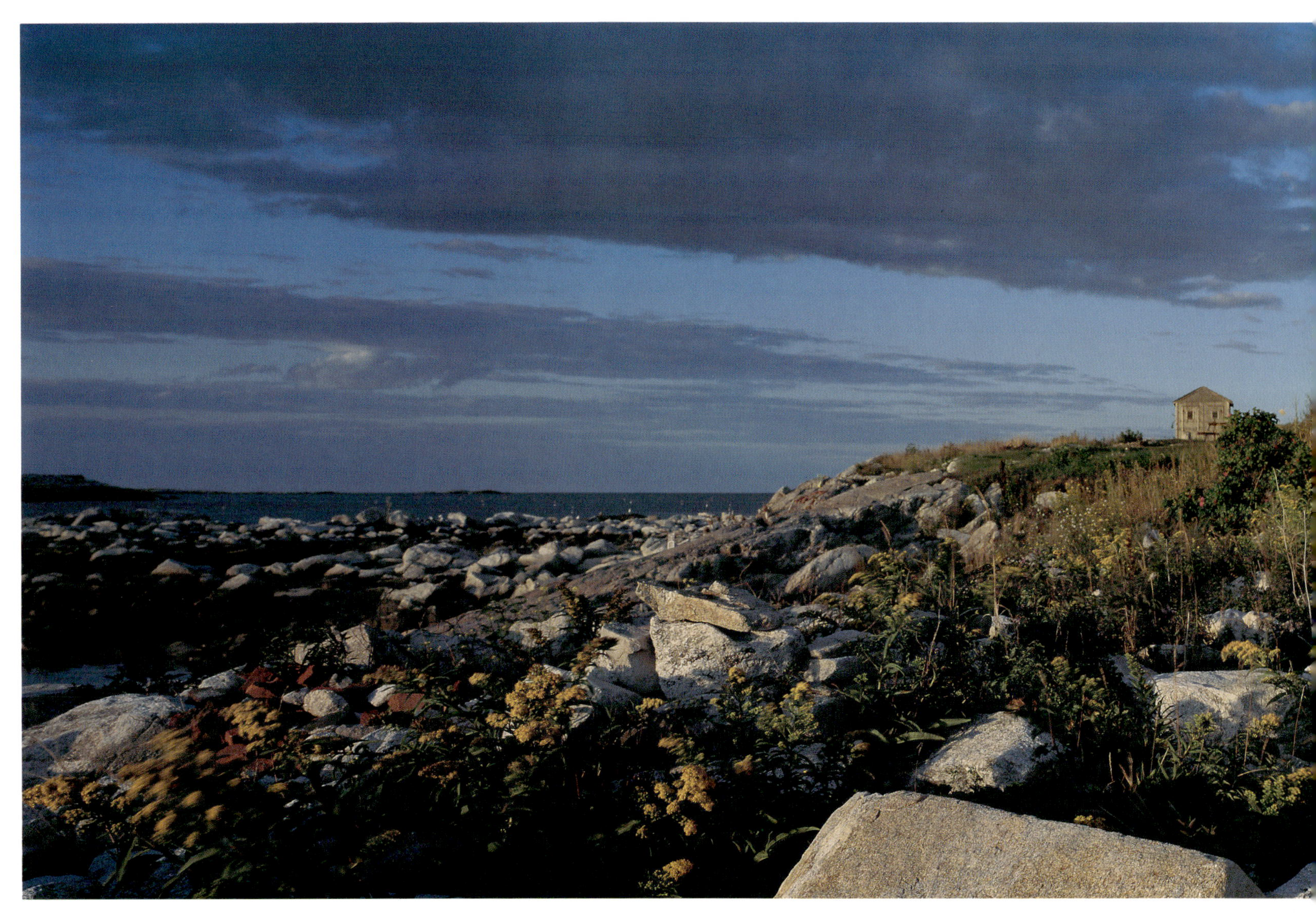

 Late afternoon, late summer, Smuttynose.

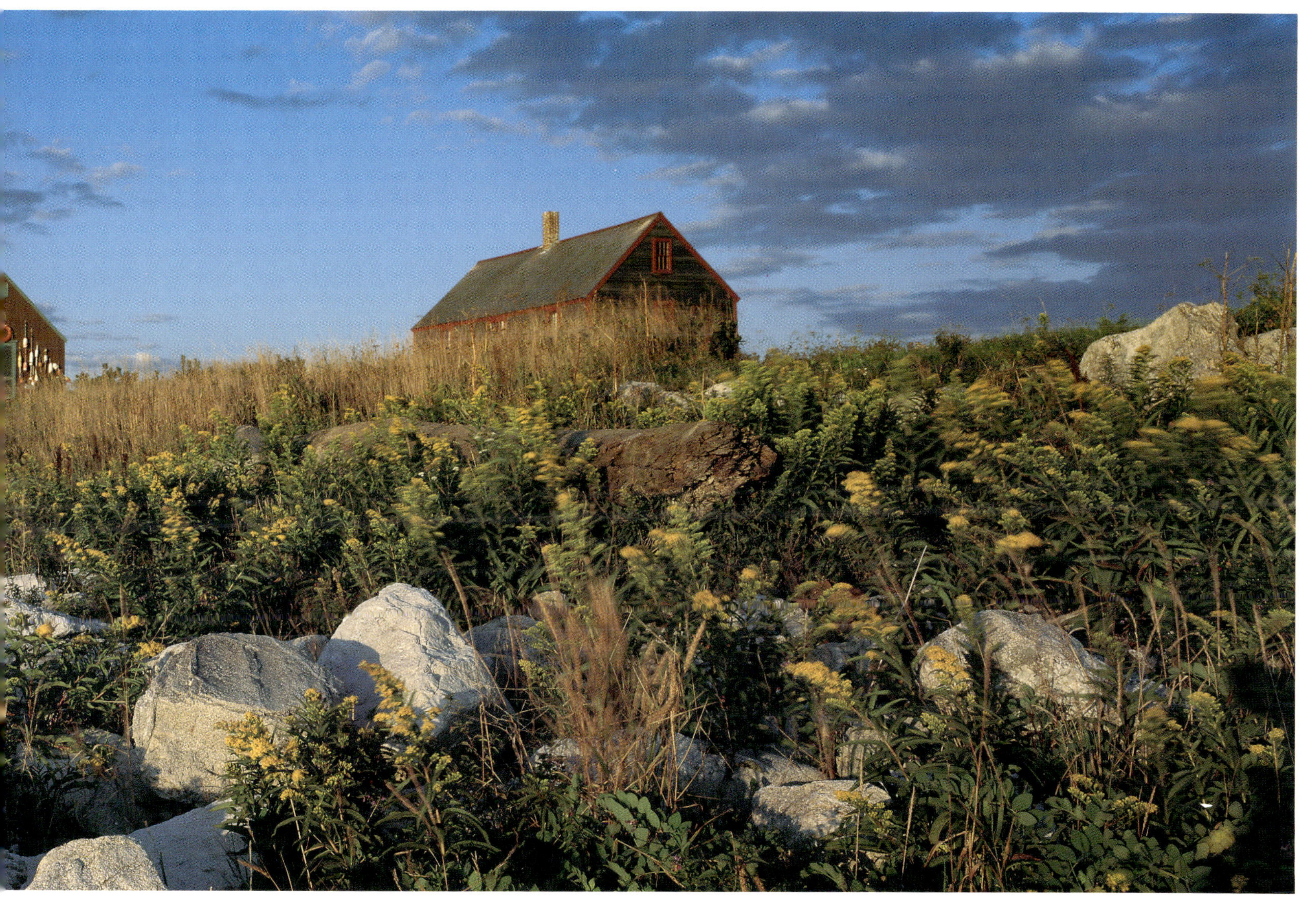

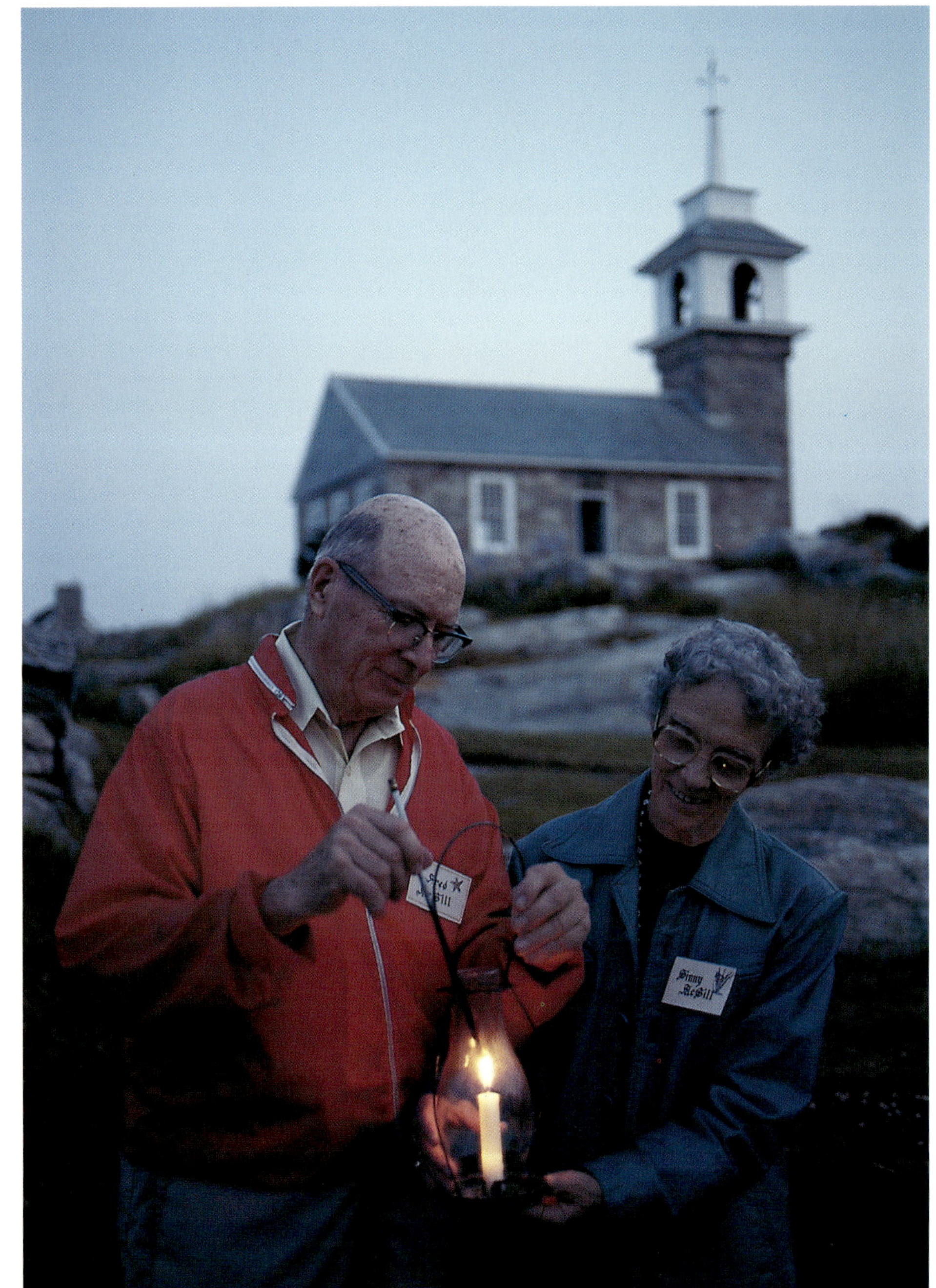

Beloved Star Islanders Fred and Ginny McGill met as young people on the island, later married, and returned each summer for over 50 years. Each evening they prepared the lanterns for the candlelight service. Now 90, Fred has spent most of 67 summers on Star.

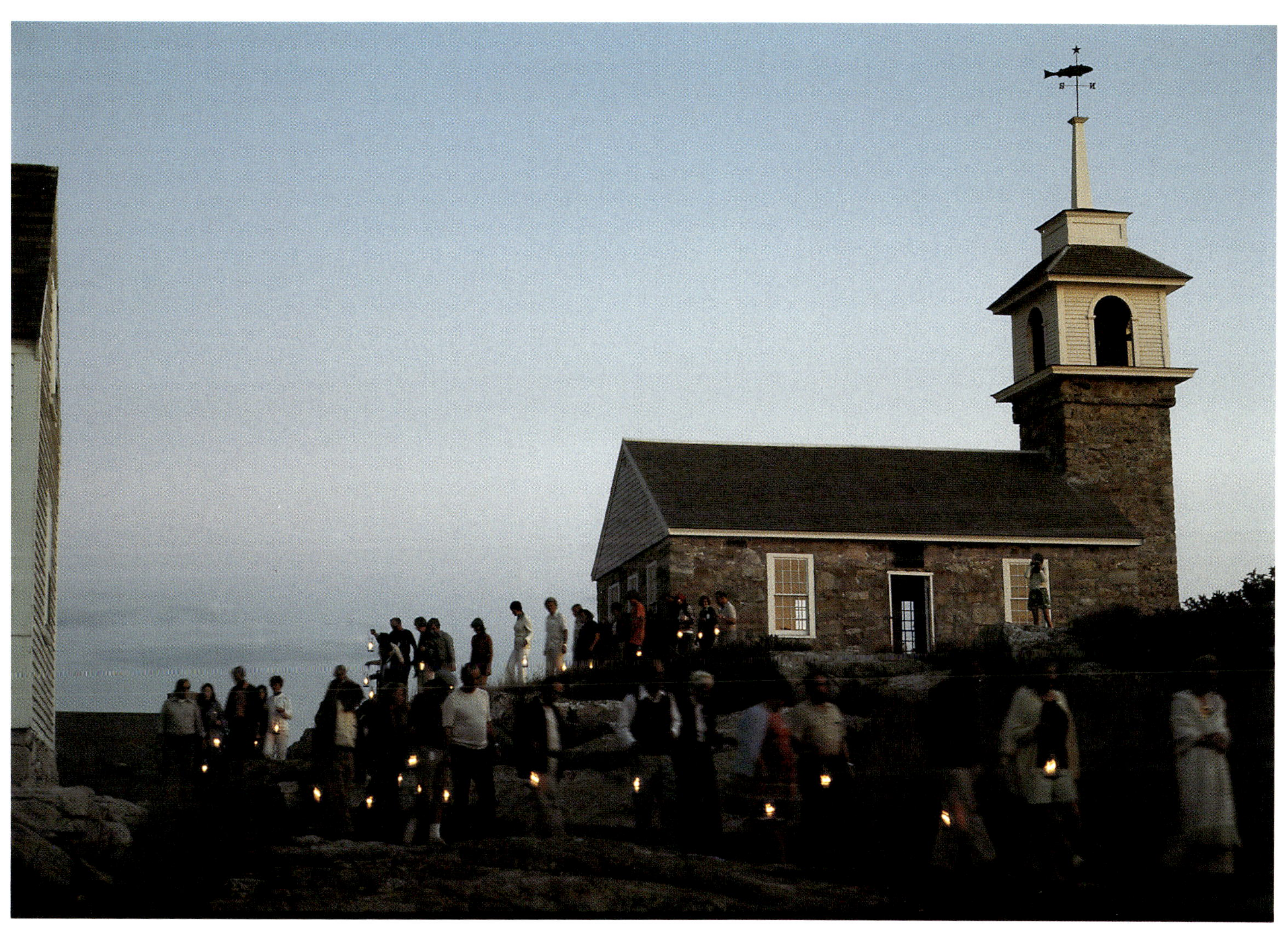

After the candlelight service, Star. This nightly summer service continues a tradition begun by early Shoalers who only had candles to light their church.

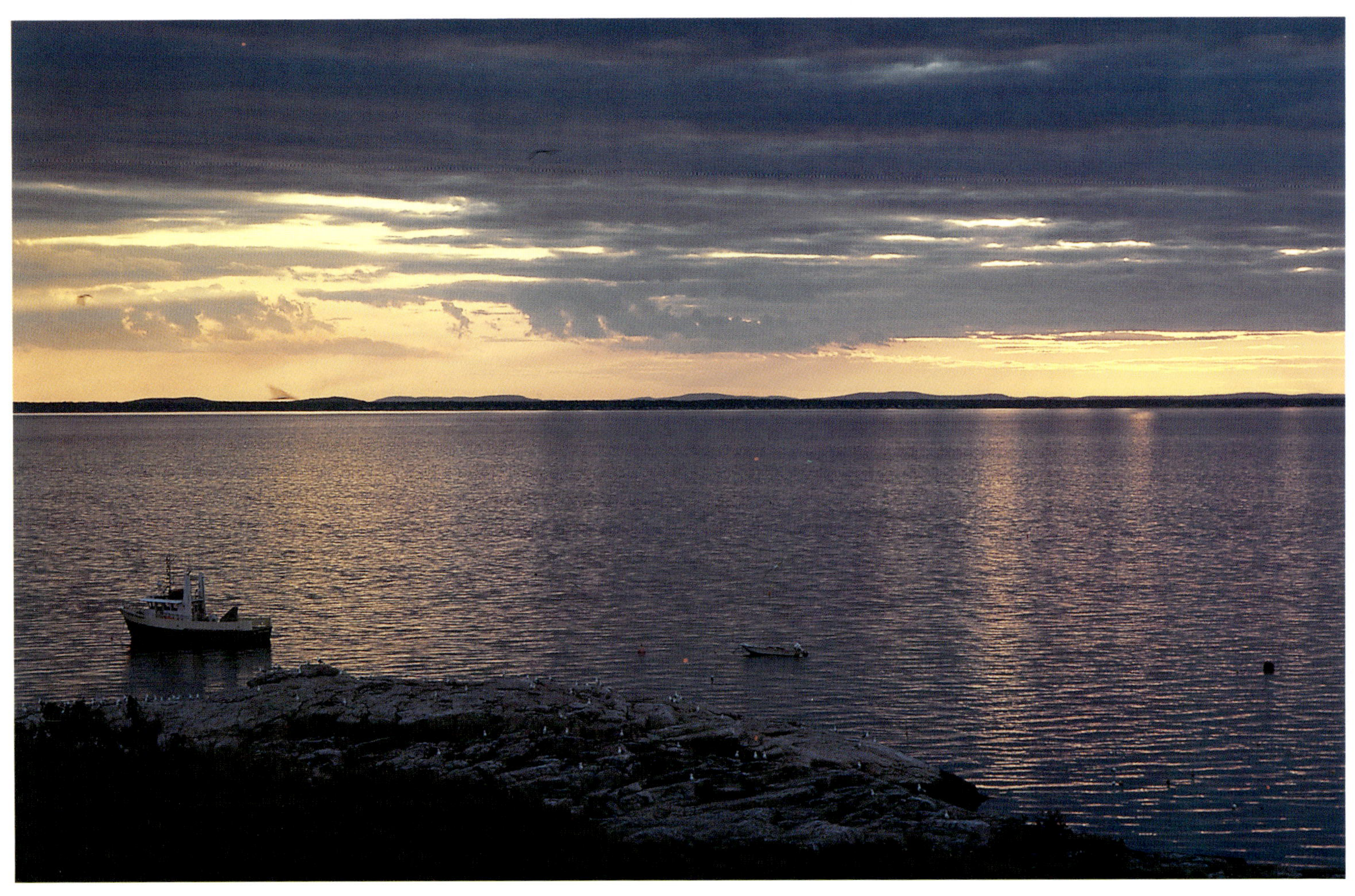

 Sunset from Appledore.

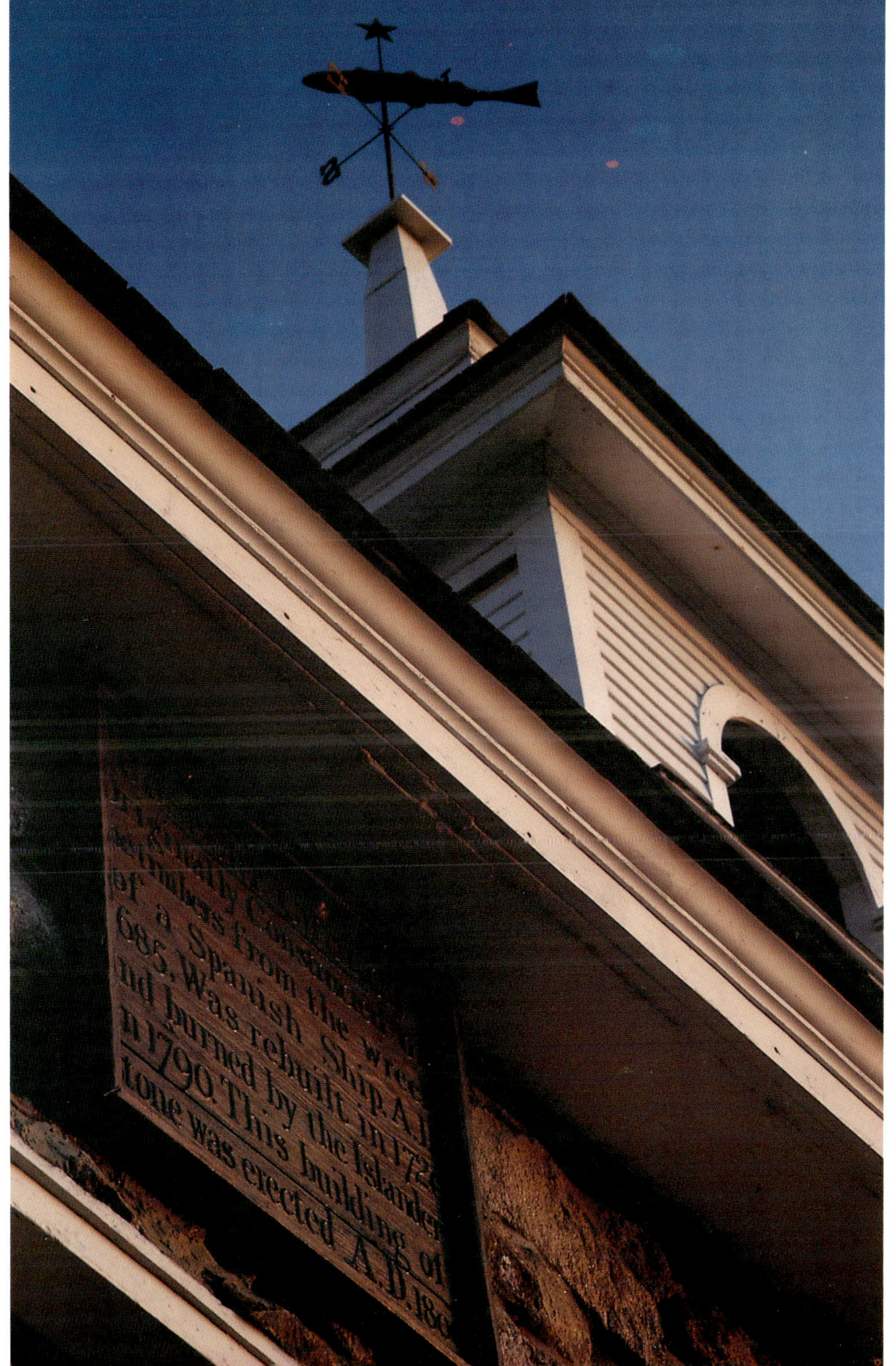

Gosport Church is the historical link between the time when year-around fishing families, served by missionaries, lived on the islands, and today's summer religious conferences.

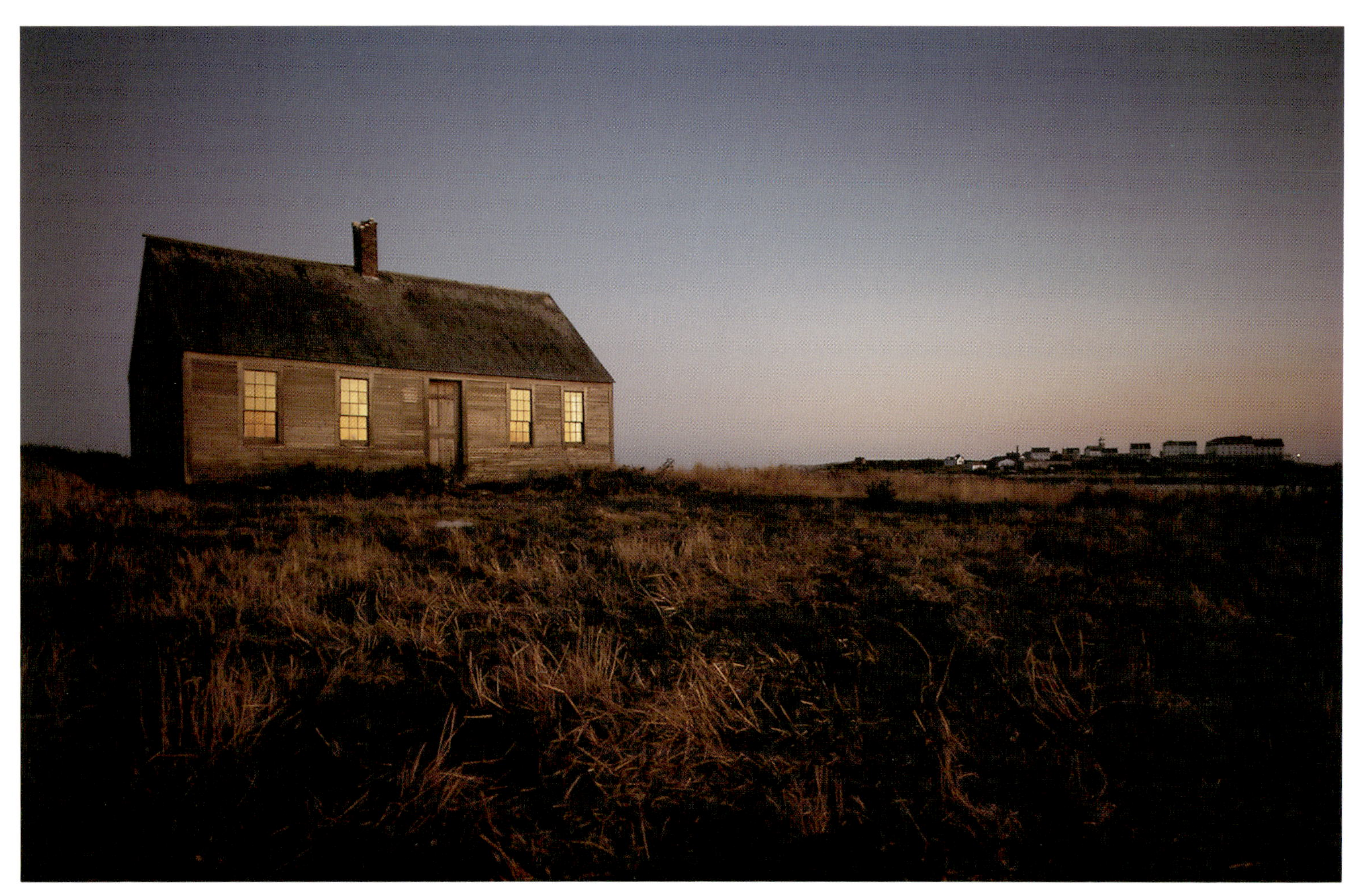

 Samuel Haley House, circa 1800, Smuttynose.

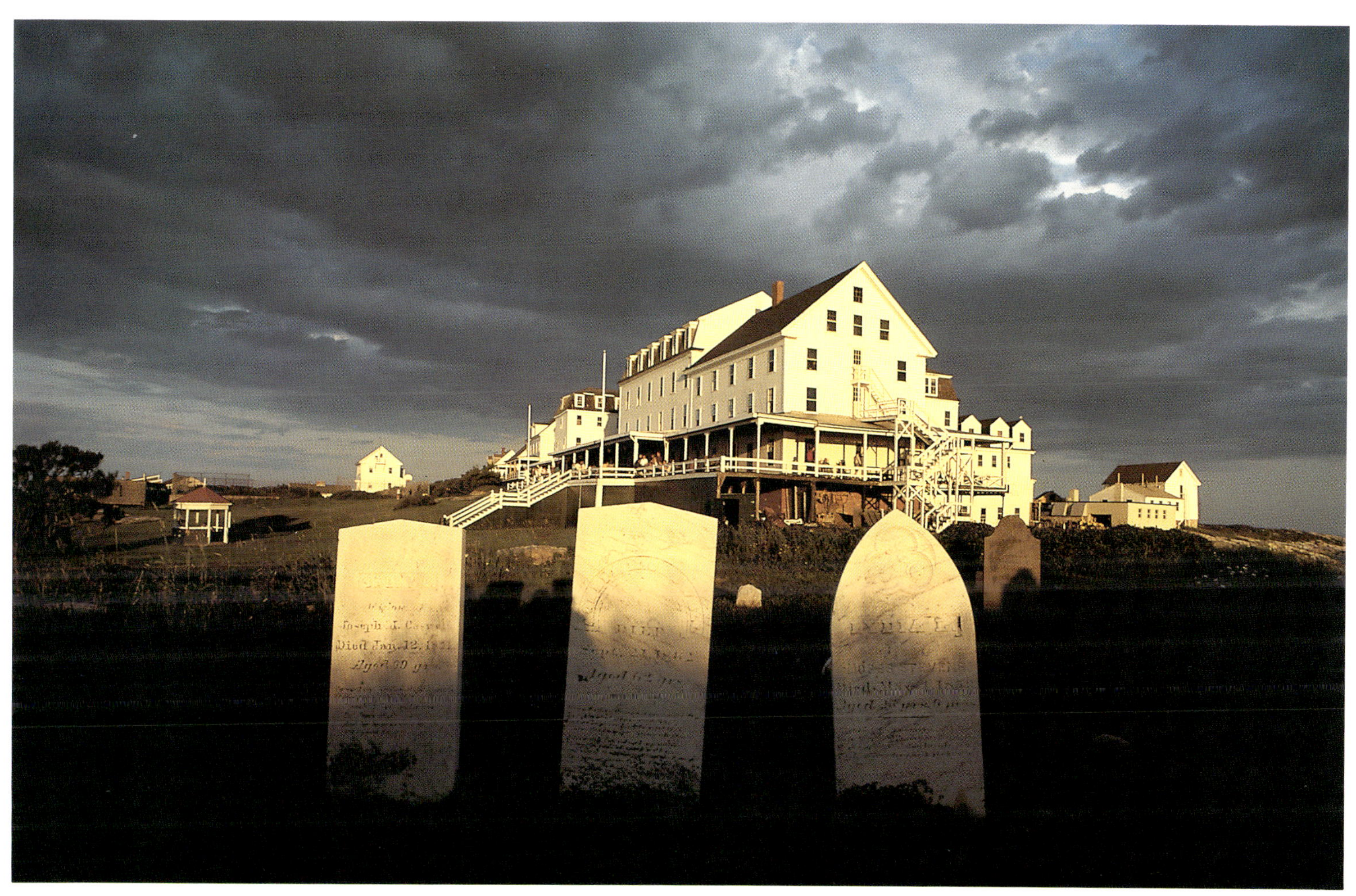

Caswell cemetery and Oceanic Hotel, Star Island.

 Sunset over White Island, from Star Island.